D0938467

THE FLOWERS OF EVIL

THE FLOWERS OF EVIL

And Other Writings

CHARLES BAUDELAIRE

TRANSLATED BY F. P. STURM,
W. J. ROBERTSON, AND JOSEPH T. SHIPLEY

INTRODUCTION BY F. P. STURM

BARNES & NOBLE
NEW YORK

Originally published in 1919

This 2008 edition published by Barnes & Noble, Inc.

Cover art: *Pink Rose with Wreath of Thorns* © John Ritter /
Images.com / Corbis

ISBN-13: 978-1-4351-0750-2

Printed and bound in the United States of America

1 3 5 5 7 9 10 8 6 4 2

Contents

LITTLE POEMS IN PROSE

POEMS IN PROSE

INTRODUCTION

I

CHARLES BAUDELAIRE WAS ONE OF THOSE WHO TAKE THE downward path which leads to salvation. There are men born to be the martyrs of the world and of their own time; men whose imagination carries them beyond all that we know or have learned to think of as law and order; who are so intoxicated with a vision of a beauty beyond the world that the world's beauty seems to them but a little paint above the face of the dead; who love God with a so consuming fire that they must praise evil for God's glory, and blaspheme His name that all sects and creeds may be melted away; who see beneath all there is of mortal loveliness, the invisible worm, feeding upon hopes and desires no less than upon the fair and perishable flesh; who are good and evil at the same time; and because the good and evil in their souls finds a so perfect instrument in the refined and tortured body of modern times, desire keener pleasure and more intolerable anguish than the world contains, and become materialists because the tortured heart cries out in denial of the soul that tortures it. Charles Baudelaire was one of these men; his art is the expression of his decadence; a study of his art is the understanding of that complex movement, that "inquietude of the Veil in the temple," as Mallarmé called it, that has changed the literature of the world; and, especially, made of poetry the subtle and delicate instrument of emotional expression it has become in our own day.

We used to hear a deal about Decadence in the arts, and now we hear as much about Symbolism, which is a flower sprung from the old corruption—but Baudelaire *is* decadence; his art is not a mere literary affectation, a mask of sorrow to be thrown aside when the curtain falls, but the voice of an imagination plunged into the contemplation of all the perverse and fallen loveliness of the world; that finds beauty most beautiful at the moment of its passing away, and regrets its perishing with a so poignant grief that it must needs follow it even into the narrow grave where those "dark comrades the worms, without ears, without eyes," whisper their secrets of terror and tell of yet another pang—

Pour ce vieux corps sans âme et mort parmi les morts.

All his life Baudelaire was a victim to an unutterable weariness, that terrible malady of the soul born out of old times to prey upon civilisations that have reached their zenith—weariness, not of life, but of living, of continuing to labour and suffer in a world that has exhausted all its emotions and has no new thing to offer. Being an artist, therefore, he took his revenge upon life by a glorification of all the sorrowful things that it is life's continual desire to forget. His poems speak sweetly of decay and death, and whisper their graveyard secrets into the ears of beauty. His men are men whom the moon has touched with her own phantasy: who love the immense ungovernable sea, the unformed and multitudinous waters; the place where they are not; the woman they will never know; and all his women are enigmatic courtesans whose beauty is a transfiguration of sin; who hide the ugliness of the soul beneath the perfection of the body. He loves them and does not love; they are cruel and indolent and full of strange perversions; they are perfumed with exotic perfumes; they sleep to the sound of viols, or fan themselves languidly in the shadow, and only he sees that it is the shadow of death.

An art like this, rooted in a so tortured perception of the beauty and ugliness of a world where the spirit is mingled indistinguishably with the flesh, almost inevitably concerns itself with material things, with all the subtle raptures the soul feels, not by abstract contemplation, for that would mean content, but through the gateway of the senses; the lust of the flesh, the delight of the eye. Sound, colour, odour, form: to him these are not the symbols that lead the soul towards the infinite: they are the soul; they are the infinite. He writes, always with a weary and laborious grace, about the abstruser and more enigmatic things of the flesh, colours and odours particularly; but, unlike those later writers who have been called realists, he apprehends, to borrow a phrase from Pater, "all those finer conditions wherein material things rise to that subtlety of operation which constitutes them spiritual, where only the finer nerve and the keener touch can follow."

In one of his sonnets he says:

Je hais la passion et l'esprit me fait mal!

and, indeed, he is a poet in whom the spirit, as modern thought understands the word, had little or no part. We feel, reading his terrible poems, that the body is indeed acutely conscious of the soul, distressfully and even angrily conscious, but its motions are not yet subdued by the soul's prophetic voice. It was to forget this voice, with its eternal *Esto memor,* that Baudelaire wrote imperishably of perishable things and their fading glory.

II

Charles Baudelaire was born at Paris, April 21st, 1821, in an old turreted house in the Rue Hautefeuille. His father, a distinguished

Baudelaire — Bios FBook
avail on Kindle

gentleman of the eighteenth-century school, seems to have passed his old-world manners on to his son, for we learn from Baudelaire's friend and biographer, Théophile Gautier, that the poet "always preserved the forms of an extreme urbanity."

At school, during his childhood, he gained many distinctions, and passed for a kind of infant prodigy; but later on, when he sat for his examination as *bachelier ès lettres,* his extreme nervousness made him appear almost an idiot. Failing miserably, he made no second attempt. Then his father died, and his mother married General Aupick, afterwards ambassador to Constantinople, an excellent man in every respect, but quite incapable of sympathising with or even of understanding the love for literature that now began to manifest itself in the mind of his stepson. All possible means were tried to turn him from literature to some more lucrative and more respectable profession. Family quarrels arose over this all-important question, and young Baudelaire, who seems to have given some real cause for offence to the stepfather whose aspirations and profession he despised, was at length sent away upon a long voyage, in the hopes that the sight of strange lands and new faces would perhaps cause him to forget the ambitions his relatives could but consider as foolish and idealistic. He sailed the Indian Seas; visited the islands of Mauritius, Bourbon, Madagascar, and Ceylon; saw the yellow waters of the sacred Ganges; stored up the memory of tropical sounds and colours and odours for use later on; and returned to Paris shortly after his twenty-first birthday, more than ever determined to be a man of letters.

His parents were in despair; no doubt quite rightly so from their point of view. Théophile Gautier, perhaps remembering the many disappointments and martyrdoms of his own sad life, defends the attitude of General Aupick in a passage where he poignantly describes the hopelessness of the profession of letters. The future author of *The Flowers of Evil,* however, was now his own master and in a position, so far as monetary matters were concerned, to follow out his own whim. He took apartments in the Hôtel Pimodan, a kind of literary lodging-house where all Bohemia met; and where Gautier and Boissard were also at that period installed. Then began that life of uninterrupted labour and meditation that has given to France her most characteristic literature, for these poems of Baudelaire's are not only original in themselves but have been the cause of originality in others; they are the root of modern French literature and much of the best English literature; they were the origin of that new method in poetry that gave Mallarmé and Verlaine to France; Yeats and some others to England. It was in the Hôtel Pimodan that Baudelaire and Gautier first met and formed one of those unfading friendships not so rare among men of letters as among men of the world; there also the "Hashish-Eaters" held the *séances* that have since become famous in the history of literature. Hashish and opium, indeed, contribute not a little to the odour of the strange *Flowers of Evil;* as also, perhaps, they contributed to Baude-laire's death from the terrible malady known as general paralysis, for he was a man who could not resist a so easy path into the world of *macabre* visions. I shall return to this question again; there is internal evidence in his writings that shows he made good literary use of these opiate-born dreams which in the end dragged him into their own abyss.

It was in 1849, when Baudelaire was twenty-eight years of age, that he made the acquaintance of the already famous Théophile Gautier, from whose admirable essay I shall presently translate a passage giving us an excellent pen-sketch of the famous poet and cynic—for Baudelaire was a cynic: he had not in the least degree the rapt expression and vague personality usually supposed to be characteristic of the poetic mood. "He recalls," wrote M. Dulamon, who knew him well, "one of those beautiful Abbés of the eigh-teenth century, so correct in their doctrine, so indulgent in their commerce with life—the Abbé de Bernis, for example. At the same time, he writes better verse, and would not have demanded at Rome the destruction of the Order of Jesuits."

That was Baudelaire exactly, suave and polished, filled with sceptical faith, cynical with the terrible cynicism of the scholar who is acutely conscious of all the morbid and gloomy secrets hidden beneath the fair exteriors of the world. Gautier, in the passage I have already mentioned, emphasises both his reserve and his cynicism:

Contrary to the somewhat loose manners of artists generally, Baudelaire prided himself upon observing the most rigid *convenances;* his courtesy, indeed, was excessive to the point of seeming affected. He measured his sentences, using only the most carefully chosen terms, and pronounced certain words in a particular manner, as though he wished to underline them and give them a mysterious importance. He had italics and capital letters in his voice. Exaggeration, much in honour at Pimodan's, he disdained as being theatrical and gross; though he himself affected paradox and excess. With a very simple, very natural, and perfectly detached air, as though retailing, *à la Prudhomme,* a newspaper paragraph about the mildness or rigour of the weather, he would advance some satanically monstrous axiom, or uphold with the coolness of ice some theory of a mathematical extravagance; for he always followed a rigorous plan in the development of his follies. His spirit was neither in words nor traits; he saw things from a particular point of view, so that their outlines were changed, as objects when one gets a bird's-eye view of them; he perceived analogies inappreciable to others, and you were struck by their fantastic logic. His rare gestures were slow and sober; he never threw his arms about, for he held southern gesticulation in horror; British coolness seemed to him to be good taste. One might describe him as a dandy who had strayed into Bohemia; though still preserving his rank, and that cult of self which characterises a man imbued with the principles of Brummel.

At this time Baudelaire was practically unknown outside his own circle of friends, writers themselves; and it was not until eight years later, in 1857, when he published his *Flowers of Evil*, that he became famous. Infamous would perhaps be a better word to describe the kind of fame he at first obtained, for every Philistine in France joined in the cry against a poet who dared to remind his readers that the grave awaits even the rich; who dared to choose the materials of his art from among the objects of death and decay; who exposed the mouldering secrecies of the grave, and painted, in the phosphorescent colours of corruption, frescoes of death and horror; who desecrated love in the sonnet entitled *Causerie*:

You are a sky of autumn, pale and rose!
But all the sea of sadness in my blood
Surges, and ebbing, leaves my lip morose
Salt with the memory of the bitter flood.

In vain your hand glides my faint bosom o'er;
That which you seek, beloved, is desecrate
By woman's tooth and talon: ah! No more
Seek in me for a heart which those dogs ate!

It is a ruin where the jackals rest,
And rend and tear and glut themselves and slay!
—A perfume swims about your naked breast,
Beauty, hard scourge of spirits, have your way!
With flame-like eyes that at bright feasts have flared
Burn up these tatters that the beasts have spared!

We can recall nothing like it in the literary history of our own country; the sensation caused by the appearance of the first series of Mr. Swinburne's *Poems and Ballads* was mild in comparison; just as Mr. Swinburne's poems were but wan derivatives from Baudelaire—at least as far as ideas are concerned; I say nothing about their beauty of expression or almost absolute mastery of technique—for it is quite obvious that the English poet was indebted to Baudelaire for all the bizarre and satanic elements in his work; as Baudelaire was indebted to Poe. Mr. Swinburne, however, is wild where Baudelaire is grave; and where Baudelaire compresses some perverse and morbid image into a single unforgettable line, Mr. Swinburne beats it into a froth of many musical lovely words, until we forget the deep sea in the shining foam.

If we call to mind the reception at first given to the black-and-white work of Aubrey Beardsley, it will give some idea of the consternation caused in France by the appearance of the *Flowers of Evil*. Beardsley, indeed, resembles Baudelaire in many ways, for he achieved in art what the other achieved in literature: the apotheosis of the horrible and grotesque, the perfecting of symbols to shadow forth intellectual sin, the tearing away of the decent veil of forgetfulness that hides our own corruption from our eyes, and his one prose romance, *Under the Hill,* unhappily incomplete at his death at the age of twenty-four, beats Baudelaire on his own ground. The four or five chapters which alone remain of this incomplete romance stand alone in literature. They are the absolute attainment of what Baudelaire more or less successfully attempted—a testament of sin. Not the sin of the flesh, the gross faults of the body that are vulgarly known as sin; but sin which is a metaphysical corruption, a depravity of pure intellect, the sin of the fallen angels in hell who cover their anguish with the sound of harps and sweet odours; who are incapable of bodily impurity, and for whom spiritual purity is the only terror. And since mortality, which is the shadow of the immortal, can comprehend spiritual and abstract things only by the analogies and correspondences which exist between them and the far reflections of them that we call reality, both Baudelaire and Beardsley, as indeed all artists who speak with tongues of spiritual truth, choose more or less actual human beings to be the shadows of the divine or satanic beings they would invoke, and make them sin delicate sins of the refined bodily sense that we may get a far-off glimpse of the Evil that is not mortal but immortal, the Spiritual Evil that has set up its black throne beside the throne of Spiritual Good, and has equal share in the shaping of the world and man.

I am not sure that Baudelaire, when he wrote this sinister poetry, had any clear idea that it was his vocation to be a prophet either of good or evil. Certainly he had no thought of founding a school of poetry, and if he made any conscious effort to bring a new method into literature, it was merely because he desired to be one of the famous writers of his country. An inspired thinker, however, whether his inspiration be mighty or small, receives his thought from a profounder source than his own physical reason, and writes to the dictation of beings outside of and greater than himself. The famous Eliphas Levi, like all the mystics who came before and after him, from Basilides the Gnostic to Blake the English visionary, taught that the poet and dreamer are the mediums of the Divine Word, and sole instruments through which the gods energise in the world of material things. The writing of a great book is the casting of a pebble into the pool of human thought; it gives rise to ever-widening circles that will reach we know not whither, and begins a chain of circumstances that may end in the destruction of kingdoms and religions and the awakening of new gods. The change wrought, directly or indirectly, by *The Flowers of Evil* alone is almost too great to be properly understood. There is perhaps not a man in Europe today whose outlook on life would not have been different had *The Flowers of Evil* never been written. The first thing that happens after the publication of such a book is the theft of its ideas and the imitation of its style by the lesser writers who labour for the multitude, and so its teaching goes from book to book, from the greater to the lesser, as the divine hierarchies emanate from Divinity, until ideas that were once paradoxical, or even blasphemous and unholy, have become mere newspaper commonplaces adopted by the numberless thousands who do not think for themselves, and the world's thought is changed completely, though by infinite slow degrees. The immediate result of Baudelaire's work was the Decadent School in French literature. Then the influence spread across the Channel, and the English Æsthetes arose to preach the gospel of imagination to the unimaginative. Both Decadence and Æstheticism, as intellectual movements, have fallen into the nadir of oblivion, and the dust lies heavy upon them, but they left a little leaven to lighten the heavy inertness of correct and academic literature; and now Symbolism, a greater movement than either, is in the ascendant, giving another turn to the wheel, and to all who think deeply about such matters it seems as though Symbolist literature is to be the literature of the future. The Decadents and Æsthetes were weak because they had no banner to fight beneath, no authority to appeal to in defence of their views, no definite gospel to preach. They were by turns morbid, hysterical, foolishly blasphemous, or weakly disgusting, but never anything for long, their one desire being to produce a thrill at any cost. If the hospital failed they went to the brothel, and when even obscenity failed to stimulate the jaded palates of their generation there was still the graveyard left. A more or less successful imitation of Baudelaire's awful verses entitled *The Corpse* has been the beginning of more than one French poet's corrupt flight across the sky of literature. That Baudelaire himself was one of their company is not an accusation, for he had genius, which his imitators, English or French, have not; and his book, even apart from the fact that it made straight the way for better things, must be

admitted to be a great and subtly wrought work of art by whoso-
ever reads it with understanding. And, moreover, his morbidness
is not at all an affectation; his poems inevitably prove the writer to
have been quite sincere in his perversion and in his decadence.

The Symbolist writers of today, though they are sprung from
him, are greater than he because they are the prophets of a faith
who believe in what they preach. They find their defence in the
writings of the mystics, and their doctrines are at the root of every
religion. They were held by the Gnostics and are in the books of
the Kabbalists and the Magi. Blake preached them and Eliphas
Levi taught them to his disciples in France, who in turn have
misunderstood and perverted them, and formed strange religions and sects of Devil-worshippers. These doctrines hold that
the visible world is the world of illusion, not of reality. Colour and
sound and perfume and all material and sensible things are but
the symbols and far-off reflections of the things that are alone
real. Reality is hidden away from us by the five senses and the
gates of death; and Reason, the blind and laborious servant of
the physical brain, deludes us into believing that we can know
anything of truth through the medium of the senses. It is through
the imagination alone that man can obtain spiritual revelation,
for imagination is the one window in the prison-house of the
flesh through which the soul can see the proud images of eternity.
And Blake, who is the authority of all English Symbolist writers,
long since formulated their creed in words that have been quoted
again and again, and must still be quoted by all who write in
defence of modern art: "The world of imagination is the world of
Eternity. It is the divine bosom into which we shall all go after
the death of the vegetated body. This world of imagination is
infinite and eternal, whereas the world of generation, or vegeta-
tion, is finite and temporal. There exist in that eternal world the
permanent realities of everything which we see reflected in this
vegetable glass of nature."

In spite of the cry against *Flowers of Evil,* Baudelaire did not lack defenders among literary men themselves; and many enthusiastic articles were written in praise of his book. Thierry not unjustly compared him to Dante, to which Barbey d'Aurevilly replied, "Baudelaire comes from hell, Dante only went there"; adding at the finish of his article: "After the *Flowers of Evil* there are only two possible ways for the poet who made them blossom: either to blow out his brains or become a Christian." Baudelaire did neither. And Victor Hugo, after reading the two poems, *The Seven Old Men* and *The Little Old Women,* wrote to Baudelaire. "You have dowered the heaven of art with one knows not what deathly gleam," he said in his letter; "you have created a new shudder." The phrase became famous, and for many years after this the creation of a new shudder was the ambition of every young French writer worth his salt.

When the first great wave of public astonishment had broken and ebbed, Baudelaire's work began to be appreciated by others than merely literary men, by all in fact who cared for careful art and subtle thinking, and before long he was admitted to be the greatest after Hugo who had written French verse. He was famous and he was unhappy. Neither glory, nor love, nor friendship—and he knew them all—could minister to the disease of that fierce mind, seeking it knew not what and never finding it; seeking it, unhappily, in the strangest excesses. He took opium to quieten his nerves when they trembled, for something to do when they did not, and made immoderate use of hashish to produce visions and heighten his phantasy. His life was a haunted weariness. Thomas de Quincey's *Confessions of an English Opium-Eater* seems to have fascinated him to a great extent, for besides imitating the vices of the author, he wrote, in imitation of his book, *The Artificial Paradises,* a monograph on the effects of opium and hashish, partly original, partly a mere translation from the *Confessions.*

He remembered his visions and sensations as an eater of drugs and made literary use of them. At the end of this book, among the *Poems in Prose,* will be found one entitled *The Double Chamber,* almost certainly written under the influence of opium, and the last verse of *The Temptation*—

> O mystic metamorphosis!
> My senses into one sense flow—
> Her voice makes perfume when she speaks,
> Her breath is music faint and low!

as well as the last six lines of that profound sonnet *Correspondences*—

> Some perfumes are as fragrant as a child,
> Sweet as the sound of hautboys, meadow-green;
> Others, corrupted, rich, exultant, wild,
> Have all the expansion of things infinite:
> As amber, incense, musk, and benzoin,
> Which sing the sense's and the soul's delight,

are certainly memories of a sensation he experienced under the influence of hashish, as recorded in *The Artificial Paradises,* where he has this curious passage:

> The senses become extraordinarily acute and fine. The eyes pierce Infinity. The ear seizes the most unseizable sounds in the midst of the shrillest noises. Hallucinations commence External objects take on monstrous appearances and show themselves under forms hitherto unknown. . . . The most singular equivocations, the most inexplicable transposition of ideas, take place. *Sounds are perceived to have a colour, and colour becomes musical.*

Baudelaire need not have gone to hashish to discover this. The mystics of all times have taught that sounds in gross matter produce

colour in subtle matter; and all who are subject to any visionary
condition know that when in trance colours will produce words of
a language whose meaning is forgotten as soon as one awakes to
normal life; but I do not think Baudelaire was a visionary. His work
shows too precise a method, and a too ordered appreciation of
the artificial in beauty. There again he is comparable to Aubrey
Beardsley, for I have read somewhere that when Beardsley was
asked if ever he saw visions, he replied, "I do not permit myself to
see them, except upon paper." The whole question of the colour
of sound is one of supreme interest to the poet, but it is too difficult and abstract a question to be written of here. A famous sonnet
by Rimbaud on the colour of the vowels has founded a school of
symbolists in France. I will content myself with quoting that—in
the original, since it loses too much by translation:

A noir, E blanc, I rouge, U vert, O bleu, voyelles,
Je dirai quelque jour vos naissances latentes,
A, noir corset velu des mouches éclatantes
Qui bourdonnent autour des puanteurs cruelles,
Golfes d'ombres; E, candeurs des vapeurs et des tentes,
Lances des glaciers fiers, rois blancs, frissons d'ombrelles;
I, poupre, sang craché; rire des lèvres belles
Dans la colère ou les ivresses pénitentes;
U, cycles, yibrements divins des mers virides,
Paix des pâtis semés d'animaux, paix des rides
Que l'alchimie imprime aux grands fronts studieux.
O, suprême clairon, plein de strideurs étranges,
Silences traversés des mondes et des anges.
—O l'Omega, rayon violet de ses yeux.

It is to be hoped that opium and hashish rendered Baudelaire
somewhat less unhappy during his life, for they certainly contributed to hasten his death. Always of an extremely neurotic
temperament, he began to break down beneath his excesses, and

shortly after the publication of *The Artificial Paradises,* which shows a considerable deterioration in his style, he removed from Paris to Brussels in the hope of building up his health by the change. At Brussels he grew worse. His speech began to fail; he was unable to pronounce certain words and stumbled over others. Hallucinations commenced, no longer the hallucinations of hashish; and his disease, rapidly establishing itself, was recognised as "general paralysis of the insane." Gautier tells how the news of his death came to Paris while he yet lived. It was false news, but prematurely true. Baudelaire lingered on for another three months; motionless and inert, his eyes the only part of him alive; unable to speak or even to write, and so died.

He left, besides *The Flowers of Evil* and *Little Poems in Prose* (his masterpieces), several volumes of critical essays, published under the titles of *Æsthetic Curiosities* and *Romantic Art; The Artificial Paradises,* and his translations of the works of Edgar Allan Poe—admirable pieces of work by which Poe actually gains.

III

Baudelaire's love of the artificial has been insisted upon by all who have studied his work, but to my mind never sufficiently insisted upon, for it was the foundation of his method. He wrote many arguments in favour of the artificial, and elaborated them into a kind of paradoxical philosophy of art. His hatred of nature and purely natural things was but a perverted form of the religious ecstasy that made the old monk pull his cowl about his eyes when he left his cell in the month of May, lest he should see the blossoming trees, and his mind be turned towards the beautiful delusions of the world. The Egyptians and the earliest of the Christians looked upon nature not as the work of the good and benevolent spirit who is the father of our souls, but as the work of the rebellious "gods of generation," who fashion beautiful things to capture the heart of man and bind his soul to earth. Blake, whom I have already quoted, hated nature in the same fashion, and held death to be the one way of escape from "the delusions of goddess Nature and her laws." Baudelaire's revolt against external things was more a revolt of the intellect than of the imagination; and he expresses it, not by desiring that the things of nature should be swept away to make room for the things of the spirit, but that they should be so changed by art that they cease to be natural. As he was of all poets the most intensely modern, holding that "modernity is one-half of art," the other half being something "eternal and immutable," he preferred, unlike Blake and his modern followers, to express himself in quite modern terms, and so wrote his famous and much misunderstood *Eloge du Maquillage* to defend his views. As was usual with him, he pushed his ideas to their extreme logical sequence, and the casual reader who picks up that extraordinary essay is in consequence quite misled as to the writer's intention.

It seems scarcely necessary at this time of day to assert that the *Eloge du Maquillage* is something more than a mere *Praise of Cosmetics*, written by a man who wished to shock his readers. It is the part expression of a theory of art, and if it is paradoxical and far-fetched it is because Baudelaire wrote at a time when French literature, in the words of M. Asselineau, "was dying of correctness," and needed very vigorous treatment indeed. If the *Eloge du Maquillage* had been more restrained in manner, if it had not been something so entirely contrary to all accepted ideas of the well-regulated citizen who never thinks a thought that somebody else has not put into his head, it might have been passed over without notice. It was written to initiate the profane; to make them think, at least; and not to raise a smile among the initiated. And moreover, it was in a manner a defence of his own work that had met with so much hatred and opposition.

He begins by attempting to prove that Nature is innately and fundamentally wrong and wicked.

charles Asselineau — (1820 - 1874)
FRIEND of Baudelaire

The greater number of errors relative to the beautiful date from the eighteenth century's false conceptions of morality. Nature was regarded in those times as the base, source, and type of all possible good and beauty. . . . If, however, we consent to refer simply to the visible facts . . . we see that Nature teaches nothing, or almost nothing. That is to say, she *forces* man to sleep, to drink, to eat, and to protect himself, well or ill, against the hostilities of the atmosphere. It is she also who moves him to kill and eat or imprison and torture his kind; for, as soon as we leave the region of necessities and needs to enter into that of luxuries and pleasures, we see that Nature is no better than a counsellor to crime. . . . Religion commands us to nourish our poor and infirm parents; Nature (the voice of our own interest) commands us to do away with them. Pass in review, analyse all that is natural, all the actions and desires of the natural man, and you will find nothing but what is horrible. All beautiful and noble things are the result of calculation. Crime, the taste for which the human animal absorbs before birth, is originally natural. Virtue, on the contrary, is *artificial*, supernatural, since there has been a necessity in all ages and among all nations for gods and prophets to preach virtue to humanity; since man alone would have been unable to discover it. Evil is done without effort, *naturally* and by fatality; good is always the product of an art.

So far the argument is straightforward and expresses what many must have thought, but Baudelaire, remembering that exaggeration is the best way of impressing one's ideas upon the unimaginative, immediately carries his argument from the moral order to the order of the beautiful, and applies it there. The result is strange enough.

I am thus led to regard personal adornment as one of the signs of the primitive nobility of the human soul. The races that our confused and perverted civilisation, with a fatuity and pride entirely laughable, treats as savages, understand as does the child the high spirituality of the toilet. The savage and the child, by their naïve love of all brilliant things, of glittering plumage and shining stuffs, and the superlative majesty of artificial forms, bear witness to their distaste for reality, and so prove, unknown to themselves, the immateriality of their souls.

Thus, with some appearance of logic, he carries his argument a step farther, and this immediately brings him to the bizarre conclusion that the more beautiful a woman naturally is, the more she should hide her natural beauty beneath the artificial charm of rouge and powder. "She performs a duty in attempting to appear magical and supernatural. She is an idol who must adorn herself to be adored." Powder and rouge and kohl, all the little artifices that shock respectability, have for their end "the creation of an abstract unity in the grain and colour of the skin." This unity brings the human being nearer to the condition of a statue—that is to say, "a divine and superior being." Red and black are the symbols of "an excessive and supernatural life." A touch of kohl "lends to the eye a more decided appearance of a window opened upon infinity"; and rouge augments the brilliance of the eye, "and adds to a beautiful feminine face the mysterious passion of the priestess." But artifice cannot make ugliness any the less ugly, nor help age to rival youth. "Who dare assign to art the sterile function of imitating nature?" Deception, if it is to have any charm, must be obvious and unashamed; it must be displayed "if not with affectation, at least with a kind of candour."

Such theories as these, if they are sincerely held, necessarily lead the theorist into the strangest bypaths of literature.

Baudelaire, like many another writer whose business is with verse, pondered so long upon the musical and rhythmical value of words that at times words became meaningless to him. He thought his own language too simple to express the complexities of poetic reverie, and dreamed of writing his poems in Latin. Not, however, in the Latin of classical times; that was too robust, too natural, too "brutal and purely epidermic," to use an expression of his own; but in the corrupt Latin of the Byzantine decadence, which he considered as "the supreme sigh of a strong being already transformed and prepared for the spiritual life."

One of these Latin poems has appeared in all editions of *The Flowers of Evil.* Though dozens as good are to be found in the Breviary of the Roman Church, "*Franciscæ Meæ Laudes*" has been included in this selection for the benefit of those curious in such matters. It is one of Baudelaire's many successful steps in the wrong direction.

IV

In almost every line of *The Flowers of Evil* one can trace the influence of Edgar Poe, and in the many places where Baudelaire has attained a pure imaginative beauty as in *The Sadness of the Moon* or *Music* or *The Death of Lovers*, it is a beauty that would have pleased the author of *Tales of the Grotesque and Arabesque*. Another kind of beauty, the beauty of death—for in Baudelaire's crucible everything is melted into loveliness—is even more directly traceable to Poe. In spite of the sonnet *Correspondences*, and in spite of his Symbolist followers of the present day, Baudelaire himself made but an imperfect use of such symbols as he had; and these he found ready to his hand in the works of the American poet. The Tomb, the symbol of death or of an intellectual darkness inhabited by the Worm, who is remorse; the Abyss, which is the despair into which the mortal part of man's mind plunges when brought into contact with dead and perishing substances; all these are borrowed from Poe. The Worm, who "devours with a kiss," occasionally becomes Time devouring life, or the Demon, "the obscure Enemy who gnaws the heart"; and when it is none of these it is the Serpent, as in that sombre poem *To a Madonna*— the Serpent beneath the feet of conquering purity. Baudelaire's imagination, however, which continually ran upon *macabre* images, loved remorse more than peace, and loved the Serpent more than the purity that would slay it, so he destroys purity with *Seven Knives* which are the *Seven Deadly Sins*, that the Serpent may live to prey upon a heart that finds no beauty in peace. Even Love is evil, for his "ancient arrows" are "crime, horror, folly," and the god Eros becomes a demon lying in wait:

> Let us love gently. Love, from his retreat
> Ambushed and shadowy, bends his fatal bow,
> And I too well his ancient arrows know:
> Crime, Horror, Folly. . . .

Gautier pretends that the poet preserved his ideal under the form of "the adorable phantom of La Beatrix, the ideal ever desired, never attained, the divine and superior beauty incarnated in an ethereal woman, spiritualised, made of light and flame and perfume, a vapour, a dream, a reflection of the seraphical world"; but when Baudelaire has a vision of this same Beatrice he sees her as one of a crowd of "cruel and curious demons" who mock at his sorrow, and she, too, mocks him, and caresses the demons who are his spiritual foes.

Baudelaire was too deeply in love with the artificial to care overmuch for the symbols he could have found among natural objects. Only once in *The Flowers of Evil* does he look upon the Moon with the eyes of a mystic; and that is when he remembers that all people of imagination are under the Moon's influence, and makes his poet hide her iridescent tear in his heart, "far from the eyes of the Sun," for the Sun is lord of material labours and therefore hostile to the dreams and reveries that are the activity of the poet. He sought more for bizarre analogies and striking metaphors than for true symbols or correspondences. He is happiest when comparing the vault of the heaven to "the lighted ceiling of a music hall," or "the black lid of the mighty pot where the human generations boil"; and when he thinks of the unfortunate and unhappy folk of the world, he does not see any hope for them in any future state; he sees, simply, "God's awful claw" stretched out to tear them. He offers pity, but no comfort.

Sometimes he has a vision of a beauty unmingled with any malevolence; but it is always evoked by sensuous and material things; perfume or music; and always it is a sorrowful loveliness he mourns or praises. Perhaps of all his poems *The Balcony* is most full of that tender and reverential melancholy we look for in a poem of love; but even it tells of a passion that has faded out of heart and mind and become beautiful only with its passing away, and not of an existing love. The other love poems—if indeed such a name can be given to *A Madrigal of Sorrow*, *The Eyes of Beauty*, *The Remorse of the Dead*, and the like—are nothing but terrible confessions of satiety, or cruelty, or terror. I have translated *The Corpse*, his most famous and most infamous poem, partly because it shows him at his worst as the others in the volume at his best, partly because it is something of the nature of a literary curiosity. A poem like *The Corpse*, which is simply an example of what may happen if any writer pushes his theories to the extreme, does not at all detract, be it said, from Baudelaire's delicate genius; for though he may not be quite worthy of a place by Dante, he has written poems that Dante might have been proud to write, and he is worthy to be set among the very greatest of the moderns, alongside Hugo and Verlaine. Read the sonnet entitled *Beauty* and you will see how he has invoked in fourteen

lines the image of a goddess, mysterious and immortal; as fair as
that Aphrodite who cast the shadow of her loveliness upon the
Golden Age; as terrible as Pallas, "the warrior maid invincible."
And as Minerva loved mortality in the person of Ulysses, so
Baudelaire's personification of Beauty loves the poets who pray
before her and gaze into her eternal eyes, watching the rising and
setting of their visionary Star in those placid mirrors.

The explanation of most of Baudelaire's morbid imaginings
is this, that he was a man haunted by terrible dream-like memories; chief among them the memory that the loveliness he had
adored in woman—the curve of a perfect cheek, the lifting of a
perfect arm in some gesture of imperial indolence, the fall of a
curl across a pale brow, all the minute and unforgettable things
that give immortality to some movement of existence—all these,
and the woman and her lover, must pass away from Time and
Space; and he, unhappily, knew nothing of the philosophy that
teaches us how all objects and events, even the most trivial—a
woman's gesture, a rose, a sigh, a fading flame, the sound that
trembles on a lute-string—find a place in Eternity when they pass
from the recognition of our senses. If he believed in the death-
lessness of man's personality he gained no comfort from his
belief. He mourned the body's decay; he was not concerned with
the soul; and no heaven less palpable than Mohammed's could
have had any reality in his imagination.

His prose is as distinguished in its manner as his verse. I think
it was Professor Saintsbury who first brought *The Little Poems in
Prose,* a selection from which is included in this volume, before
the notice of English readers in an essay written many years ago.
I am writing this in France, far from the possibility of consulting
any English books, but if my memory serves me rightly he considered the prose of these prose poems to be as perfect as literature
can be. I think he said, "they go as far as prose can go." They need
no other introduction than themselves, for they are perfect of

their kind, and not different in thought from the more elabo-
rately wrought poems of *The Flowers of Evil.* Some of them, as for
instance *Every Man His Chimæra*, are as classical and as universally
true as the myths and symbolisms of the Old Testament; and all of
them, I think, are worthy of a place in that book the Archangel
of the Presence will consult when all is weighed in the balance—
the book written by man himself, the record of his deep and
shallow imaginings. Baudelaire wrote them, he said, because he
had dreamed, "in his days of ambition," "of a miracle of poetical
prose, musical without rhythm and without rhyme." His attitude
of mind was always so natural to him that he never thought it
necessary to make any excuse for the spirit of his art or the drear
philosophy he preached; unless a short notice printed in the first
edition of his poems, but withdrawn from the second edition,
explaining that "faithful to his dolorous programme, the author
of *The Flowers of Evil*, as a perfect comedian, has had to mould his
spirit to all sophisms as to all corruptions," can be considered as
an excuse. From whatever point of view we regard him: whether
we praise his art and blame his philosophy, or blame his art and
praise his philosophy, he is as difficult to analyse as he is difficult
to give a place to, for we have none with whom to compare him,
or very few, too few to be of service to the critic. His art is like the
pearl, a beautiful product of disease, and to blame it is like blam-
ing the pearl.

He looked upon life very much as Poe, whom he so admired,
looked upon it: with the eye of a sensitive spectator in some
gloomy vault of the Spanish Inquisition, where beauty was upon
the rack; he was horrified, but unable to turn from a sight that
fascinated him by its very terror. His moments of inspiration are
haunted by the consciousness that evil beings, clothed with horror as with a shroud, are ever lingering about the temple of life
and awaiting an opportunity to enter. He was like a man who
awakens trembling from a nightmare, afraid of the darkness, and

unable to believe the dawn may be less hopeless than the midnight. Perhaps he was haunted, as many artists and all mystics, by a fear of madness and of the unseen world of evil shapes that sanity hides from us and madness reveals. Is there a man, is there a writer, especially, who has not at times been conscious of a vague and terrible fear that the whole world of visible nature is but a comfortable illusion that may fade away in a moment and leave him face-to-face with the horror that has visited him in dreams? The old occult writers held that the evil thoughts of others beget phantoms in the air that can make themselves bodies out of our fear, and haunt even our waking moments. These were the shapes of terror that haunted Baudelaire. Shelley, too, writes of them with as profound a knowledge as the magical writer of the *Middle Ages*. They come to haunt his Prometheus.

> Blackening the birth of day with countless wings,
> And hollow underneath, like death.

They are the elemental beings who dwell beside the soul of the dreamer and the poet, "like a vain loud multitude"; turning life into death and all beautiful thoughts into poems like *The Flowers of Evil*, or into tales like the satanic reveries of Edgar Poe.

> We are the ministers of pain, and fear,
> And disappointment, and mistrust, and hate,
> And clinging crime; and as lean dogs pursue
> Through wood and lake some struck and sobbing fawn,
> We track all things that weep, and bleed, and live,
> When the great King betrays them to our will.

And every man gives them of the substance of his imagination to clothe them in prophetic shapes that are the images of his destiny:

From our victim's destined agony
The shade which is our form invests us round,
Else we are shapeless as our mother Night.

The greatest of all poets conquer their dreams; others, who are great, but not of the greatest, are conquered by them, and Baudelaire was one of these. There is a passage in the works of Edgar Poe that Baudelaire may well have pondered as he laboured at his translation, for it reveals the secret of his life:

There are moments when, even to the sober eye of reason, the world of our sad humanity may assume the semblance of a hell; but the imagination of man is no Carathis to explore with impunity its every cavern. Alas! The grim legion of sepulchral terrors cannot be regarded as altogether fanciful; but, like the demons in whose company Afrasiab made his voyage down the Oxus, they must sleep or they will devour us—they must be suffered to slumber or we perish.

THE FLOWERS OF EVIL

TRANSLATED BY F. P. STURM AND
W. J. ROBERTSON

THE DANCE OF DEATH

Carrying bouquet, and handkerchief, and gloves,
Proud of her height as when she lived, she moves
With all the careless and high-stepping grace,
And the extravagant courtesan's thin face.

Was slimmer waist e'er in a ball-room wooed?
Her floating robe, in royal amplitude,
Falls in deep folds around a dry foot, shod
With a bright flower-like shoe that gems the sod.

The swarms that hum about her collar-bones
As the lascivious streams caress the stones,
Conceal from every scornful jest that flies,
Her gloomy beauty; and her fathomless eyes

Are made of shade and void; with flowery sprays
Her skull is wreathed artistically, and sways,
Feeble and weak, on her frail vertebræ.
O charm of nothing decked in folly! They

Who laugh and name you a Caricature,
They see not, they whom flesh and blood allure,
The nameless grace of every bleached, bare bone,
That is most dear to me, tall skeleton!

Come you to trouble with your potent sneer
The feast of Life! Or are you driven here,
To Pleasure's Sabbath, by dead lusts that stir
And goad your moving corpse on with a spur?

Or do you hope, when sing the violins,
And the pale candle-flame lights up our sins,
To drive some mocking nightmare far apart,
And cool the flame hell lighted in your heart?

Fathomless well of fault and foolishness!
Eternal alembic of antique distress!
Still o'er the curved, white trellis of your sides
The sateless, wandering serpent curls and glides.

And truth to tell, I fear lest you should find,
Among us here, no lover to your mind;
Which of these hearts beat for the smile you gave?
The charms of horror please none but the brave.

Your eyes' black gulf, where awful broodings stir,
Brings giddiness; the prudent reveller
Sees, while a horror grips him from beneath,
The eternal smile of thirty-two white teeth.

For he who has not folded in his arms
A skeleton, nor fed on graveyard charms,
Recks not of furbelow, or paint, or scent,
When Horror comes the way that Beauty went.

O irresistible, with fleshless face,
Say to these dancers in their dazzled race:
"Proud lovers with the paint above your bones,
Ye shall taste death, musk-scented skeletons!

Withered Antinoüs, dandies with plump faces,
Ye varnished cadavers, and grey Lovelaces,
Ye go to lands unknown and void of breath,
Drawn by the rumour of the Dance of Death.

From Seine's cold quays to Ganges' burning stream,
The mortal troupes dance onward in a dream;
They do not see, within the opened sky,
The Angel's sinister trumpet raised on high.

In every clime and under every sun,
Death laughs at ye, mad mortals, as ye run;
And oft perfumes herself with myrrh, like ye;
And mingles with your madness, irony!"

THE BEACONS

RUBENS, oblivious garden of indolence,
    Pillow of cool flesh where no man dreams of love,
Where life flows forth in troubled opulence,
    As airs in heaven and seas in ocean move.

LEONARD DA VINCI, sombre and fathomless glass,
    Where lovely angels with calm lips that smile,
Heavy with mystery, in the shadow pass,
    Among the ice and pines that guard some isle.

REMBRANDT, sad hospital that a murmuring fills,
    Where one tall crucifix hangs on the walls,
Where every tear-drowned prayer some woe distils,
    And one cold, wintry ray obliquely falls.

Strong MICHELANGELO, a vague far place
    Where mingle Christs with pagan Hercules;
Thin phantoms of the great through twilight pace,
    And tear their shroud with clenched hands void of ease.

milo of CROTONA STATUE

The fighter's anger, the faun's impudence,
　　Thou makest of all these a lovely thing;
Proud heart, sick body, mind's magnificence:
　　PUGET, the convict's melancholy king.

(1620-1694) FR, Baroque ARTIST et al

(1684-
1721)

WATTEAU, the carnival of illustrious hearts,
　　Fluttering like moths upon the wings of chance;
Bright lustres light the silk that flames and darts,
　　And pour down folly on the whirling dance.

GOYA, a nightmare full of things unknown;
　　The fœtus witches broil on Sabbath night;
Old women at the mirror; children lone
　　Who tempt old demons with their limbs delight.

1798-1863

DELACROIX, lake of blood ill angels haunt,
　　Where ever-green, o'ershadowing woods arise;
Under the surly heaven strange fanfares chaunt
　　And pass, like one of Weber's strangled sighs.

A CURSE   Liturgical Hymn of P

And malediction, blasphemy and groan,
　　Ecstasies, cries, Te Deums, and tears of brine,
Are echoes through a thousand labyrinths flown;
　　For mortal hearts an opiate divine;

A shout cried by a thousand sentinels,
　　An order from a thousand bugles tossed,
A beacon o'er a thousand citadels,
　　A call to huntsmen in deep woodlands lost.

It is the mightiest witness that could rise
　　To prove our dignity, O Lord, to Thee;
This sob that rolls from age to age, and dies
　　Upon the verge of Thy Eternity!

THE SADNESS OF THE MOON

The Moon more indolently dreams tonight
Than a fair woman on her couch at rest,
Caressing, with a hand distraught and light,
Before she sleeps, the contour of her breast.

Upon her silken avalanche of down,
Dying she breathes a long and swooning sigh;
And watches the white visions past her flown,
Which rise like blossoms to the azure sky.

And when, at times, wrapped in her languor deep,
Earthward she lets a furtive tear-drop flow,
Some pious poet, enemy of sleep,

Takes in his hollow hand the tear of snow
Whence gleams of iris and of opal start,
And hides it from the Sun, deep in his heart.

THE BALCONY

Mother of memories, mistress of mistresses,
    O thou, my pleasure, thou, all my desire,
Thou shalt recall the beauty of caresses,
    The charm of evenings by the gentle fire,
Mother of memories, mistress of mistresses!

The eves illumined by the burning coal,
    The balcony where veiled rose-vapour clings—
How soft your breast was then, how sweet your soul!
    Ah, and we said imperishable things,
Those eves illumined by the burning coal.

Lovely the suns were in those twilights warm,
    And space profound, and strong life's pulsing flood,

In bending o'er you, queen of every charm,
    I thought I breathed the perfume in your blood.
The suns were beauteous in those twilights warm.

The film of night flowed round and over us,
    And my eyes in the dark did your eyes meet;
I drank your breath, ah! Sweet and poisonous,
    And in my hands fraternal slept your feet—
Night, like a film, flowed round and over us.

I can recall those happy days forgot,
    And see, with head bowed on your knees, my past.
Your languid beauties now would move me not
    Did not your gentle heart and body cast
The old spell of those happy days forgot.

Can vows and perfumes, kisses infinite,
    Be reborn from the gulf we cannot sound;
As rise to heaven suns once again made bright
    After being plunged in deep seas and profound?
Ah, vows and perfumes, kisses infinite!

THE SICK MUSE

Poor Muse, alas, what ails thee, then, today?
Thy hollow eyes with midnight visions burn,
Upon thy brow in alternation play,
Folly and Horror, cold and taciturn.

Have the green lemure and the goblin red,
Poured on thee love and terror from their urn?
Or with despotic hand the nightmare dread
Deep plunged thee in some fabulous Minturne?

Would that thy breast where so deep thoughts arise,
Breathed forth a healthful perfume with thy sighs;
Would that thy Christian blood ran wave by wave

In rhythmic sounds the antique numbers gave,
When Phœbus shared his alternating reign
With mighty Pan, lord of the ripening grain.

THE VENAL MUSE

Muse of my heart, lover of palaces,
    When January comes with wind and sleet,
During the snowy eve's long wearinesses,
    Will there be fire to warm thy violet feet?

Wilt thou reanimate thy marble shoulders
    In the moon-beams that through the window fly?
Or when thy purse dries up, thy palace moulders,
    Reap the far star-gold of the vaulted sky?

For thou, to keep thy body to thy soul,
Must swing a censer, wear a holy stole,
    And chaunt Te Deums with unbelief between.

Or, like a starving mountebank, expose
Thy beauty and thy tear-drowned smile to those
    Who wait thy jests to drive away thy spleen.

THE EVIL MONK

The ancient cloisters on their lofty walls
    Had holy Truth in painted frescoes shown,
And, seeing these, the pious in those halls
    Felt their cold, lone austereness less alone.

At that time when Christ's seed flowered all around,
　　More than one monk, forgotten in his hour,
Taking for studio the burial-ground,
　　Glorified Death with simple faith and power.

And my soul is a sepulchre where I,
Ill cenobite, have spent eternity:
　　On the vile cloister walls no pictures rise.

O when may I cast off this weariness,
And make the pageant of my old distress
　　For these hands labour, pleasure for these eyes?

THE TEMPTATION

The Demon, in my chamber high,
　　This morning came to visit me,
And, thinking he would find some fault,
　　He whispered: "I would know of thee

Among the many lovely things
　　That make the magic of her face,
Among the beauties, black and rose,
　　That make her body's charm and grace,

Which is most fair?" Thou didst reply
　　To the Abhorred, O soul of mine:
"No single beauty is the best
　　When she is all one flower divine.

When all things charm me I ignore
　　Which one alone brings most delight;
She shines before me like the dawn,
　　And she consoles me like the night.

The harmony is far too great,
    That governs all her body fair.
For impotence to analyse
    And say which note is sweetest there.

O mystic metamorphosis!
    My senses into one sense flow—
Her voice makes perfume when she speaks,
    Her breath is music faint and low!"

THE IRREPARABLE

Can we suppress the old Remorse
    Who bends our heart beneath his stroke,
Who feeds, as worms feed on the corse,
    Or as the acorn on the oak?
Can we suppress the old Remorse?

Ah, in what philtre, wine, or spell,
    May we drown this our ancient foe,
Destructive glutton, gorging well,
    Patient as the ants, and slow?
What wine, what philtre, or what spell?

Tell it, enchantress, if you can,
    Tell me, with anguish overcast,
Wounded, as a dying man,
    Beneath the swift hoofs hurrying past.
Tell it, enchantress, if you can,

To him the wolf already tears
    Who sees the carrion pinions wave
This broken warrior who despairs
    To have a cross above his grave—
This wretch the wolf already tears.

Can one illume a leaden sky,
Or tear apart the shadowy veil
Thicker than pitch, no star on high,
Not one funereal glimmer pale?
Can one illume a leaden sky?

Hope lit the windows of the Inn,
But now that shining flame is dead;
And how shall martyred pilgrims win
Along the moonless road they tread?
Satan has darkened all the Inn!

Witch, do you love accursèd hearts?
Say, do you know the reprobate?
Know you Remorse, whose venomed darts
Make souls the targets for their hate?
Witch, do you know accursèd hearts?

The Might-have-been with tooth accursed
Gnaws at the piteous souls of men,
The deep foundations suffer first,
And all the structure crumbles then
Beneath the bitter tooth accursed.

II

Often, when seated at the play,
And sonorous music lights the stage,
I see the frail hand of a Fay
With magic dawn illume the rage
Of the dark sky. Oft at the play

A being made of gauze and fire
Casts to the earth a Demon great.

And my heart, whence all hopes expire,
　　Is like a stage where I await,
In vain, the Fay with wings of fire!

A FORMER LIFE

Long since, I lived beneath vast porticoes,
By many ocean-sunsets tinged and fired,
Where mighty pillars, in majestic rows,
Seemed like basaltic caves when day expired.

The rolling surge that mirrored all the skies
Mingled its music, turbulent and rich,
Solemn and mystic, with the colours which
The setting sun reflected in my eyes.

And there I lived amid voluptuous calms,
In splendours of blue sky and wandering wave,
Tended by many a naked, perfumed slave,

Who fanned my languid brow with waving palms.
They were my slaves—the only care they had
To know what secret grief had made me sad.

DON JUAN IN HADES

When Juan sought the subterranean flood,
　　And paid his obolus on the Stygian shore,
Charon, the proud and sombre beggar, stood
　　With one strong, vengeful hand on either oar.

With open robes and bodies agonised,
　　Lost women writhed beneath that darkling sky;
There were sounds as of victims sacrificed:
　　Behind him all the dark was one long cry.

And Sganarelle, with laughter, claimed his pledge;
 Don Luis, with trembling finger in the air,
Showed to the souls who wandered in the sedge
 The evil son who scorned his hoary hair.

Shivering with woe, chaste Elvira the while,
 Near him untrue to all but her till now,
Seemed to beseech him for one farewell smile
 Lit with the sweetness of the first soft vow.

And clad in armour, a tall man of stone
 Held firm the helm, and clove the gloomy flood;
But, staring at the vessel's track alone,
 Bent on his sword the unmoved hero stood.

THE LIVING FLAME

They pass before me, these Eyes full of light,
Eyes made magnetic by some angel wise;
The holy brothers pass before my sight,
And cast their diamond fires in my dim eyes.

They keep me from all sin and error grave,
They set me in the path whence Beauty came;
They are my servants, and I am their slave,
And all my soul obeys the living flame.

Beautiful Eyes that gleam with mystic light
As candles lighted at full noon; the sun
Dims not your flame phantastical and bright.

You sing the dawn; they celebrate life done;
Marching you chaunt my soul's awakening hymn,
Stars that no sun has ever made grow dim!

CORRESPONDENCES

In Nature's temple living pillars rise,
    And words are murmured none have understood,
    And man must wander through a tangled wood
Of symbols watching him with friendly eyes.

As long-drawn echoes heard far-off and dim
    Mingle to one deep sound and fade away;
    Vast as the night and brilliant as the day,
Colour and sound and perfume speak to him.

Some perfumes are as fragrant as a child,
    Sweet as the sound of hautboys, meadow-green;
Others, corrupted, rich, exultant, wild,

Have all the expansion of things infinite:
    As amber, incense, musk, and benzoin,
Which sing the sense's and the soul's delight.

THE FLASK

There are some powerful odours that can pass
Out of the stoppered flagon; even glass
To them is porous. Oft when some old box
Brought from the East is opened and the locks
And hinges creak and cry; or in a press
In some deserted house, where the sharp stress
Of odours old and dusty fills the brain;
An ancient flask is brought to light again,
And forth the ghosts of long-dead odours creep.
There, softly trembling in the shadows, sleep
A thousand thoughts, funereal chrysalides,
Phantoms of old the folding darkness hides,
Who make faint flutterings as their wings unfold,
Rose-washed and azure-tinted, shot with gold.

A memory that brings languor flutters here:
The fainting eyelids droop, and giddy Fear
Thrusts with both hands the soul towards the pit
Where, like a Lazarus from his winding-sheet,
Arises from the gulf of sleep a ghost
Of an old passion, long since loved and lost.
So I, when vanished from man's memory
Deep in some dark and sombre chest I lie,
An empty flagon they have cast aside,
Broken and soiled, the dust upon my pride,
Will be your shroud, beloved pestilence!
The witness of your might and virulence,
Sweet poison mixed by angels; bitter cup
Of life and death my heart has drunken up!

REVERSIBILITY

Angel of gaiety, have you tasted grief?
    Shame and remorse and sobs and weary spite,
    And the vague terrors of the fearful night
That crush the heart up like a crumpled leaf?
Angel of gaiety, have you tasted grief?

Angel of kindness, have you tasted hate?
    With hands clenched in the shade and tears of gall,
    When Vengeance beats her hellish battle-call,
And makes herself the captain of our fate,
Angel of kindness, have you tasted hate?

Angel of health, did ever you know pain,
    Which like an exile trails his tired footfalls
    The cold length of the white infirmary walls,
With lips compressed, seeking the sun in vain?
Angel of health, did ever you know pain?

Angel of beauty, do you wrinkles know?
    Know you the fear of age, the torment vile
    Of reading secret horror in the smile
Of eyes your eyes have loved since long ago?
Angel of beauty, do you wrinkles know?

Angel of happiness, and joy, and light,
    Old David would have asked for youth afresh
    From the pure touch of your enchanted flesh;
I but implore your prayers to aid my plight,
Angel of happiness, and joy, and light.

THE EYES OF BEAUTY

You are a sky of autumn, pale and rose;
But all the sea of sadness in my blood
Surges, and ebbing, leaves my lips morose,
Salt with the memory of the bitter flood.

In vain your hand glides my faint bosom o'er,
That which you seek, beloved, is desecrate
By woman's tooth and talon; ah, no more
Seek in me for a heart which those dogs ate.

It is a ruin where the jackals rest,
And rend and tear and glut themselves and slay—
A perfume swims about your naked breast!

Beauty, hard scourge of spirits, have your way!
With flame-like eyes that at bright feasts have flared
Burn up these tatters that the beasts have spared!

SONNET OF AUTUMN

They say to me, thy clear and crystal eyes:
    "Why dost thou love me so, strange lover mine?"

Be sweet, be still! My heart and soul despise
    All save that antique brute-like faith of thine;

And will not bare the secret of their shame
    To thee whose hand soothes me to slumbers long,
Nor their black legend write for thee in flame!
    Passion I hate, a spirit does me wrong.

Let us love gently. Love, from his retreat,
Ambushed and shadowy, bends his fatal bow,
And I too well his ancient arrows know:

Crime, horror, folly. O pale Marguerite,
Thou art as I, a bright sun fallen low,
O my so white, my so cold Marguerite.

THE REMORSE OF THE DEAD

O shadowy Beauty mine, when thou shalt sleep
    In the deep heart of a black marble tomb;
When thou for mansion and for bower shalt keep
    Only one rainy cave of hollow gloom;

And when the stone upon thy trembling breast,
    And on thy straight sweet body's supple grace,
Crushes thy will and keeps thy heart at rest,
    And holds those feet from their adventurous race;

Then the deep grave, who shares my reverie,
(For the deep grave is aye the poet's friend)
During long nights when sleep is far from thee,

Shall whisper: "Ah, thou didst not comprehend
The dead wept thus, thou woman frail and weak"—
And like remorse the worm shall gnaw thy cheek.

THE GHOST

Softly as brown-eyed Angels rove
I will return to thy alcove,
And glide upon the night to thee,
Treading the shadows silently.

And I will give to thee, my own,
Kisses as icy as the moon,
And the caresses of a snake
Cold gliding in the thorny brake.

And when returns the livid morn
Thou shalt find all my place forlorn
And chilly, till the falling night.

Others would rule by tenderness
Over thy life and youthfulness,
But I would conquer thee by fright!

TO A MADONNA

(An Ex-Voto in the Spanish taste.)

Madonna, mistress, I would build for thee
An altar deep in the sad soul of me;
And in the darkest corner of my heart,
From mortal hopes and mocking eyes apart,
Carve of enamelled blue and gold a shrine
For thee to stand erect in, Image divine!
And with a mighty Crown thou shalt be crowned
Wrought of the gold of my smooth Verse, set round
With starry crystal rhymes; and I will make,
O mortal maid, a Mantle for thy sake,
And weave it of my jealousy, a gown
Heavy, barbaric, stiff, and weighted down
With my distrust, and broider round the hem
Not pearls, but all my tears in place of them.

And then thy wavering, trembling robe shall be
All the desires that rise and fall in me
From mountain-peaks to valleys of repose,
Kissing thy lovely body's white and rose.
For thy humiliated feet divine,
Of my Respect I'll make thee Slippers fine
Which, prisoning them within a gentle fold,
Shall keep their imprint like a faithful mould.
And if my art, unwearying and discreet,
Can make no Moon of Silver for thy feet
To have for Footstool, then thy heel shall rest
Upon the snake that gnaws within my breast,
Victorious Queen of whom our hope is born!
And thou shalt trample down and make a scorn
Of the vile reptile swollen up with hate.
And thou shalt see my thoughts, all consecrate,
Like candles set before thy flower-strewn shrine,
O Queen of Virgins, and the taper-shine
Shall glimmer star-like in the vault of blue,
With eyes of flame forever watching you.
While all the love and worship in my sense
Will be sweet smoke of myrrh and frankincense.
Ceaselessly up to thee, white peak of snow,
My stormy spirit will in vapours go!

And last, to make thy drama all complete,
That love and cruelty may mix and meet,
I, thy remorseful torturer, will take
All the Seven Deadly Sins, and from them make
In darkest joy, Seven Knives, cruel-edged and keen,
And like a juggler choosing, O my Queen,
That spot profound whence love and mercy start,
I'll plunge them all within thy panting heart!

THE SKY

Where'er he be, on water or on land,
 Under pale suns or climes that flames enfold;
One of Christ's own, or of Cythera's band,
 Shadowy beggar or Crœsus rich with gold;

Citizen, peasant, student, tramp; whate'er
 His little brain may be, alive or dead;
Man knows the fear of mystery everywhere,
 And peeps, with trembling glances, overhead.

The heaven above? A strangling cavern wall;
The lighted ceiling of a music-hall
 Where every actor treads a bloody soil—

The hermit's hope; the terror of the sot;
The sky: the black lid of the mighty pot
 Where the vast human generations boil!

SPLEEN

I'm like some king in whose corrupted veins
Flows agèd blood; who rules a land of rains;
Who, young in years, is old in all distress;
Who flees good counsel to find weariness
Among his dogs and playthings, who is stirred
Neither by hunting-hound nor hunting-bird;
Whose weary face emotion moves no more
E'en when his people die before his door.
His favourite Jester's most fantastic wile
Upon that sick, cruel face can raise no smile;
The courtly dames, to whom all kings are good,
Can lighten this young skeleton's dull mood
No more with shameless toilets. In his gloom
Even his lilied bed becomes a tomb.

The sage who takes his gold essays in vain
To purge away the old corrupted strain,
His baths of blood, that in the days of old
The Romans used when their hot blood grew cold,
Will never warm this dead man's bloodless pains,
For green Lethean water fills his veins.

THE OWLS

Under the overhanging yews,
The dark owls sit in solemn state,
Like stranger gods; by twos and twos
Their red eyes gleam. They meditate.

Motionless thus they sit and dream
Until that melancholy hour
When, with the sun's last fading gleam,
The nightly shades assume their power.

From their still attitude the wise
Will learn with terror to despise
All tumult, movement, and unrest;

For he who follows every shade,
Carries the memory in his breast,
Of each unhappy journey made.

BIEN LOIN D'ICI

Here is the chamber consecrate,
Wherein this maiden delicate,
And enigmatically sedate,

Fans herself while the moments creep,
Upon her cushions half-asleep,
And hears the fountains plash and weep.

Dorothy's chamber undefiled.
The winds and waters sing afar
Their song of sighing strange and wild
To lull to sleep the petted child.

From head to foot with subtle care,
Slaves have perfumed her delicate skin
With odorous oils and benzoin.
And flowers faint in a corner there.

CONTEMPLATION

Thou, O my Grief, be wise and tranquil still,
The eve is thine which even now drops down,
To carry peace or care to human will,
And in a misty veil enfolds the town.

While the vile mortals of the multitude,
By pleasure, cruel tormentor, goaded on,
Gather remorseful blossoms in light mood—
Grief, place thy hand in mine, let us be gone

Far from them. Lo, see how the vanished years,
In robes outworn lean over heaven's rim;
And from the water, smiling through her tears,

Remorse arises, and the sun grows dim;
And in the east, her long shroud trailing light,
List, O my grief, the gentle steps of Night.

TO A BROWN BEGGAR-MAID

White maiden with the russet hair,
Whose garments, through their holes, declare
That poverty is part of you,
    And beauty too.

To me, a sorry bard and mean,
Your youthful beauty, frail and lean,
With summer freckles here and there,
    Is sweet and fair.

Your sabots tread the roads of chance,
And not one queen of old romance
Carried her velvet shoes and lace
    With half your grace.

In place of tatters far too short
Let the proud garments worn at Court
Fall down with rustling fold and pleat
    About your feet;

In place of stockings, worn and old,
Let a keen dagger all of gold
Gleam in your garter for the eyes
    Of roués wise;

Let ribbons carelessly untied
Reveal to us the radiant pride
Of your white bosom purer far
    Than any star;

Let your white arms uncovered shine,
Polished and smooth and half divine;
And let your elfish fingers chase
    With riotous grace

The purest pearls that softly glow,
The sweetest sonnets of Belleau,
Offered by gallants ere they fight
    For your delight;

And many fawning rhymers who
Inscribe their first thin book to you
Will contemplate upon the stair
    Your slipper fair;

And many a page who plays at cards,
And many lords and many bards,
Will watch your going forth, and burn
    For your return;

And you will count before your glass
More kisses than the lily has;
And more than one Valois will sigh
    When you pass by.

But meanwhile you are on the tramp,
Begging your living in the damp,
Wandering mean streets and alleys o'er,
    From door to door;

And shilling bangles in a shop
Cause you with eager eyes to stop,
And I, alas, have not a sou
    To give to you.

Then go, with no more ornament,
Pearl, diamond, or subtle scent,
Than your own fragile naked grace
    And lovely face.

THE SWAN

I

Andromache, I think of you! The stream,
The poor, sad mirror where in bygone days
Shone all the majesty of your widowed grief,

The lying Simoïs flooded by your tears,
Made all my fertile memory blossom forth
As I passed by the new-built Carrousel.
Old Paris is no more (a town, alas,
Changes more quickly than man's heart may change);
Yet in my mind I still can see the booths;
The heaps of brick and rough-hewn capitals;
The grass; the stones all over-green with moss;
The *débris*, and the square-set heaps of tiles.

There a menagerie was once outspread;
And there I saw, one morning at the hour
When toil awakes beneath the cold, clear sky,
And the road roars upon the silent air,
A swan who had escaped his cage, and walked
On the dry pavement with his webby feet,
And trailed his spotless plumage on the ground.
And near a waterless stream the piteous swan
Opened his beak, and bathing in the dust
His nervous wings, he cried (his heart the while
Filled with a vision of his own fair lake):
"O water, when then wilt thou come in rain?
Lightning, when wilt thou glitter?"
                                    Sometimes yet
I see the hapless bird—strange, fatal myth—
Like him that Ovid writes of, lifting up
Unto the cruelly blue, ironic heavens,
With stretched, convulsive neck a thirsty face,
As though he sent reproaches up to God!

II

Paris may change; my melancholy is fixed.
New palaces, and scaffoldings, and blocks,
And suburbs old, are symbols all to me

Whose memories are as heavy as a stone.
And so, before the Louvre, to vex my soul,
The image came of my majestic swan
With his mad gestures, foolish and sublime,
As of an exile whom one great desire
Gnaws with no trace. And then I thought of you,
Andromache! Torn from your hero's arms;
Beneath the hand of Pyrrhus in his pride;
Bent o'er an empty tomb in ecstasy;
Widow of Hector—wife of Helenus!
And of the negress, wan and phthisical,
Tramping the mud, and with her haggard eyes
Seeking beyond the mighty walls of fog
The absent palm-trees of proud Africa;
Of all who lose that which they never find;
Of all who drink of tears; all whom grey grief
Gives suck to as the kindly wolf gave suck;
Of meagre orphans who like blossoms fade.
And one old Memory like a crying horn
Sounds through the forest where my soul is lost . . .
I think of sailors on some isle forgotten;
Of captives; vanquished . . . and of many more.

THE SEVEN OLD MEN

O swarming city, city full of dreams,
Where in full day the spectre walks and speaks;
Mighty colossus, in your narrow veins
My story flows as flows the rising sap.

One morn, disputing with my tired soul,
And like a hero stiffening all my nerves,
I trod a suburb shaken by the jar
Of rolling wheels, where the fog magnified

The houses either side of that sad street,
So they seemed like two wharves the ebbing flood
Leaves desolate by the riverside. A mist,
Unclean and yellow, inundated space—
A scene that would have pleased an actor's soul.

Then suddenly an aged man, whose rags
Were yellow as the rainy sky, whose looks
Should have brought alms in floods upon his head,
Without the misery gleaming in his eye,
Appeared before me; and his pupils seemed
To have been washed with gall; the bitter frost
Sharpened his glance; and from his chin a beard
Sword-stiff and ragged, Judas-like stuck forth.
He was not bent but broken: his backbone
Made a so true right angle with his legs,
That, as he walked, the tapping stick which gave
The finish to the picture, made him seem
Like some infirm and stumbling quadruped
Or a three-legged Jew. Through snow and mud
He walked with troubled and uncertain gait,
As though his sabots trod upon the dead,
Indifferent and hostile to the world.

His double followed him: tatters and stick
And back and eye and beard, all were the same;
Out of the same Hell, indistinguishable,
These centenarian twins, these spectres odd,
Trod the same pace toward some end unknown.
To what fell complot was I then exposed?
Humiliated by what evil chance?
For as the minutes one by one went by
Seven times I saw this sinister old man
Repeat his image there before my eyes!

Let him who smiles at my inquietude,
Who never trembled at a fear like mine,
Know that in their decrepitude's despite
These seven old hideous monsters had the mien
Of beings immortal.

             Then, I thought, must I,
Undying, contemplate the awful eighth;
Inexorable, fatal, and ironic double;
Disgusting Phoenix, father of himself
And his own son? In terror then I turned
My back upon the infernal band, and fled
To my own place, and closed my door; distraught
And like a drunkard who sees all things twice,
With feverish troubled spirit, chilly and sick,
Wounded by mystery and absurdity!

In vain my reason tried to cross the bar,
The whirling storm but drove her back again;
And my soul tossed, and tossed, an outworn wreck,
Mastless, upon a monstrous, shoreless sea.

THE LITTLE OLD WOMEN

I

Deep in the tortuous folds of ancient towns,
Where all, even horror, to enchantment turns,
I watch, obedient to my fatal mood,
For the decrepit, strange and charming beings,
The dislocated monsters that of old
Were lovely women—Lais or Eponine!
Hunchbacked and broken, crooked though they be,
Let us still love them, for they still have souls.
They creep along wrapped in their chilly rags,

Beneath the whipping of the wicked wind,
They tremble when an omnibus rolls by,
And at their sides, a relic of the past,
A little flower-embroidered satchel hangs.
They trot about, most like to marionettes;
They drag themselves, as does a wounded beast;
Or dance unwillingly as a clapping bell
Where hangs and swings a demon without pity.

Though they be broken they have piercing eyes,
That shine like pools where water sleeps at night;
The astonished and divine eyes of a child
Who laughs at all that glitters in the world.
Have you not seen that most old women's shrouds
Are little like the shroud of a dead child?
Wise Death, in token of his happy whim,
Wraps old and young in one enfolding sheet.
And when I see a phantom, frail and wan,
Traverse the swarming picture that is Paris,
It ever seems as though the delicate thing
Trod with soft steps towards a cradle new.
And then I wonder, seeing the twisted form,
How many times must workmen change the shape
Of boxes where at length such limbs are laid?
These eyes are wells brimmed with a million tears;
Crucibles where the cooling metal pales—
Mysterious eyes that are strong charms to him
Whose lifelong nurse has been austere Disaster.

II

The lovesick vestal of the old "Frasciti";
Priestess of Thalia, alas! Whose name
Only the prompter knows and he is dead;

Bygone celebrities that in bygone days
The Tivoli o'ershadowed in their bloom;
All charm me; yet among these beings frail
Three, turning pain to honey-sweetness, said
To the Devotion that had lent them wings:
"Lift me, O powerful Hippogriffe, to the skies"—
One by her country to despair was driven;
One by her husband overwhelmed with grief;
One wounded by her child, Madonna-like;
Each could have made a river with her tears.

III

Oft have I followed one of these old women,
One among others, when the falling sun
Reddened the heavens with a crimson wound—
Pensive, apart, she rested on a bench
To hear the brazen music of the band,
Played by the soldiers in the public park
To pour some courage into citizens' hearts,
On golden eves when all the world revives.
Proud and erect she drank the music in,
The lively and the warlike call to arms;
Her eyes blinked like an ancient eagle's eyes;
Her forehead seemed to await the laurel crown!

IV

Thus you do wander, uncomplaining Stoics,
Through all the chaos of the living town:
Mothers with bleeding hearts, saints, courtesans,
Whose names of yore were on the lips of all;
Who were all glory and all grace, and now
None know you; and the brutish drunkard stops,
Insulting you with his derisive love;

And cowardly urchins call behind your back.
Ashamed of living, withered shadows all,
With fear-bowed backs you creep beside the walls,
And none salute you, destined to loneliness!
Refuse of Time ripe for Eternity!
But I, who watch you tenderly afar,
With unquiet eyes on your uncertain steps,
As though I were your father, I—O wonder!
Unknown to you taste secret, hidden joy.
I see your maiden passions bud and bloom,
Sombre or luminous, and your lost days
Unroll before me while my heart enjoys
All your old vices, and my soul expands
To all the virtues that have once been yours.
Ruined! And my sisters! O congenerate hearts,
Octogenarian Eves o'er whom is stretched
God's awful claw, where will you be tomorrow?

A MADRIGAL OF SORROW

What do I care though you be wise?
    Be sad, be beautiful; your tears
But add one more charm to your eyes,
As streams to valleys where they rise;
    And fairer every flower appears

After the storm. I love you most
    When joy has fled your brow downcast;
When your heart is in horror lost,
And o'er your present like a ghost
    Floats the dark shadow of the past.

I love you when the teardrop flows,
    Hotter than blood, from your large eye;

When I would hush you to repose
Your heavy pain breaks forth and grows
    Into a loud and tortured cry.

And then, voluptuousness divine!
    Delicious ritual and profound!
I drink in every sob like wine,
And dream that in your deep heart shine
    The pearls wherein your eyes were drowned.

I know your heart, which overflows
    With outworn loves long cast aside,
Still like a furnace flames and glows,
And you within your breast enclose
    A damnèd soul's unbending pride;

But till your dreams without release
    Reflect the leaping flames of hell;
Till in a nightmare without cease
You dream of poison to bring peace,
    And love cold steel and powder well;

And tremble at each opened door,
    And feel for every man distrust,
And shudder at the striking hour—
Till then you have not felt the power
    Of Irresistible Disgust.

My queen, my slave, whose love is fear,
    When you awaken shuddering,
Until that awful hour be here,
You cannot say at midnight drear:
    "I am your equal, O my King!"

MIST AND RAIN

Autumns and winters, springs of mire and rain,
Seasons of sleep, I sing your praises loud,
For thus I love to wrap my heart and brain
In some dim tomb beneath a vapoury shroud

In the wide plain where revels the cold wind,
Through long nights when the weathercock whirls round,
More free than in warm summer day my mind
Lifts wide her raven pinions from the ground.

Unto a heart filled with funereal things
That since old days hoar frosts have gathered on,
Naught is more sweet, O pallid, queenly springs,

Than the long pageant of your shadows wan,
Unless it be on moonless eves to weep
On some chance bed and rock our griefs to sleep.

SUNSET

Fair is the sun when first he flames above,
    Flinging his joy down in a happy beam;
And happy he who can salute with love
    The sunset far more glorious than a dream.

Flower, stream, and furrow! I have seen them all
    In the sun's eye swoon like one trembling heart—
Though it be late let us with speed depart
    To catch at least one last ray ere it fall!

But I pursue the fading god in vain,
For conquering Night makes firm her dark domain,
    Mist and gloom fall, and terrors glide between,

And graveyard odours in the shadow swim,
And my faint footsteps on the marsh's rim,
    Bruise the cold snail and crawling toad unseen.

THE CORPSE

Remember, my Beloved, what thing we met
    By the roadside on that sweet summer day;
There on a grassy couch with pebbles set,
    A loathsome body lay.

The wanton limbs stiff-stretched into the air,
    Steaming with exhalations vile and dank,
In ruthless cynic fashion had laid bare
    The swollen side and flank.

On this decay the sun shone hot from heaven
    As though with chemic heat to broil and burn,
And unto Nature all that she had given
    A hundredfold return.

The sky smiled down upon the horror there
    As on a flower that opens to the day;
So awful an infection smote the air,
    Almost you swooned away.

The swarming flies hummed on the putrid side,
    Whence poured the maggots in a darkling stream,
That ran along these tatters of life's pride
    With a liquescent gleam.

And like a wave the maggots rose and fell,
    The murmuring flies swirled round in busy strife:
It seemed as though a vague breath came to swell
    And multiply with life

The hideous corpse. From all this living world
    A music as of wind and water ran,
Or as of grain in rhythmic motion swirled
        By the swift winnower's fan.

And then the vague forms like a dream died out,
    Or like some distant scene that slowly falls
Upon the artist's canvas, that with doubt
        He only half recalls.

A homeless dog behind the boulders lay
    And watched us both with angry eyes forlorn,
Waiting a chance to come and take away
        The morsel she had torn.

   .   .   .   .

And you, even you, will be like this drear thing,
    A vile infection man may not endure;
Star that I yearn to! Sun that lights my spring!
        O passionate and pure!

Yes, such will you be, Queen of every grace!
    When the last sacramental words are said;
And beneath grass and flowers that lovely face
        Moulders among the dead.

Then, O Belovèd, whisper to the worm
    That crawls up to devour you with a kiss,
That I still guard in memory the dear form
        Of love that comes to this!

AN ALLEGORY

Here is a woman, richly clad and fair,
Who in her wine dips her long, heavy hair;
Love's claws, and that sharp poison which is sin,

Are dulled against the granite of her skin.
Death she defies, Debauch she smiles upon,
For their sharp scythe-like talons every one
Pass by her in their all-destructive play;
Leaving her beauty till a later day.
Goddess she walks; sultana in her leisure;
She has Mohammed's faith that heaven is pleasure,
And bids all men forget the world's alarms
Upon her breast, between her open arms.
She knows, and she believes, this sterile maid,
Without whom the world's onward dream would fade,
That bodily beauty is the supreme gift
Which may from every sin the terror lift.
Hell she ignores, and Purgatory defies;
And when black Night shall roll before her eyes,
She will look straight in Death's grim face forlorn,
Without remorse or hate—as one new-born.

THE ACCURSED

Like pensive herds at rest upon the sands,
    These to the sea-horizons turn their eyes;
Out of their folded feet and clinging hands
    Bitter sharp tremblings and soft languors rise.

Some tread the thicket by the babbling stream,
    Their hearts with untold secrets ill at ease;
Calling the lover of their childhood's dream,
    They wound the green bark of the shooting trees.

Others like sisters wander, grave and slow,
    Among the rocks haunted by spectres thin,
Where Antony saw as larvæ surge and flow
    The veined bare breasts that tempted him to sin.

Some, when the resinous torch of burning wood
    Flares in lost pagan caverns dark and deep,
Call thee to quench the fever in their blood,
    Bacchus, who singest old remorse to sleep!

Then there are those the scapular bedights,
    Whose long white vestments hide the whip's red stain,
Who mix, in sombre woods on lonely nights,
    The foam of pleasure with the tears of pain.

O virgins, demons, monsters, martyrs! Ye
    Who scorn whatever actual appears;
Saints, satyrs, seekers of Infinity,
    So full of cries, so full of bitter tears;

Ye whom my soul has followed into hell,
    I love and pity, O sad sisters mine,
Your thirsts unquenched, your pains no tongue can tell,
    And your great hearts, those urns of love divine!

LA BEATRICE

In a burnt, ashen land, where no herb grew,
I to the winds my cries of anguish threw;
And in my thoughts, in that sad place apart,
Pricked gently with the poignard o'er my heart.
Then in full noon above my head a cloud
Descended tempest-swollen, and a crowd
Of wild, lascivious spirits huddled there,
The cruel and curious demons of the air,
Who coldly to consider me began;
Then, as a crowd jeers some unhappy man,
Exchanging gestures, winking with their eyes—
I heard a laughing and a whispering rise:

"Let us at leisure contemplate this clown,
This shadow of Hamlet aping Hamlet's frown,
With wandering eyes and hair upon the wind.
Is't not a pity that this empty mind,
This tramp, this actor out of work, this droll,
Because he knows how to assume a rôle
Should dream that eagles and insects, streams and woods,
Stand still to hear him chaunt his dolorous moods?
Even unto us, who made these ancient things,
The fool his public lamentation sings."

With pride as lofty as the towering cloud,
I would have stilled these clamouring demons loud,
And turned in scorn my sovereign head away
Had I not seen—O sight to dim the day!
There in the middle of the troupe obscene
The proud and peerless beauty of my Queen!
She laughed with them at all my dark distress,
And gave to each in turn a vile caress.

THE SOUL OF WINE

One eve in the bottle sang the soul of wine:
　　"Man, unto thee, dear disinherited,
I sing a song of love and light divine—
　　Prisoned in glass beneath my seals of red.

"I know thou labourest on the hill of fire,
　　In sweat and pain beneath a flaming sun,
To give the life and soul my vines desire,
　　And I am grateful for thy labours done.

"For I find joys unnumbered when I lave
　　The throat of man by travail long outworn,

And his hot bosom is a sweeter grave
    Of sounder sleep than my cold caves forlorn.

"Hearest thou not the echoing Sabbath sound?
    The hope that whispers in my trembling breast?
Thy elbows on the table! Gaze around;
    Glorify me with joy and be at rest.

"To thy wife's eyes I'll bring their long-lost gleam,
    I'll bring back to thy child his strength and light,
To him, life's fragile athlete I will seem
    Rare oil that firms his muscles for the fight.

"I flow in man's heart as ambrosia flows;
    The grain the eternal Sower casts in the sod—
From our first loves the first fair verse arose,
    Flower-like aspiring to the heavens and God!"

THE WINE OF LOVERS

    Space rolls today her splendour round!
    Unbridled, spurless, without bound,
    Mount we upon the wings of wine
    For skies fantastic and divine!

    Let us, like angels tortured by
    Some wild delirious phantasy,
    Follow the far-off mirage born
    In the blue crystal of the morn.

    And gently balanced on the wing
    Of the wild whirlwind we will ride,
    Rejoicing with the joyous thing.

My sister, floating side by side,
Fly we unceasing whither gleams
The distant heaven of my dreams.

THE DEATH OF LOVERS

There shall be couches whence faint odours rise,
    Divans like sepulchres, deep and profound;
Strange flowers that bloomed beneath diviner skies
    The deathbed of our love shall breathe around.

And guarding their last embers till the end,
    Our hearts shall be the torches of the shrine,
And their two leaping flames shall fade and blend
    In the twin mirrors of your soul and mine.

And through the eve of rose and mystic blue
A beam of love shall pass from me to you,
Like a long sigh charged with a last farewell;

And later still an angel, flinging wide
The gates, shall bring to life with joyful spell
The tarnished mirrors and the flames that died.

THE DEATH OF THE POOR

Death is consoler and Death brings to life;
    The end of all, the solitary hope;
We, drunk with Death's elixir, face the strife,
    Take heart, and mount till eve the weary slope.

Across the storm, the hoarfrost, and the snow,
    Death on our dark horizon pulses clear;
Death is the famous hostel we all know,
    Where we may rest and sleep and have good cheer.

Death is an angel whose magnetic palms
Bring dreams of ecstasy and slumberous calms
To smooth the beds of naked men and poor.

Death is the mystic granary of God;
The poor man's purse; his fatherland of yore;
The Gate that opens into heavens untrod!

GYPSIES TRAVELLING

The tribe prophetic with the eyes of fire
Went forth last night; their little ones at rest
Each on his mother's back, with his desire
Set on the ready treasure of her breast.

Laden with shining arms the men-folk tread
By the long wagons where their goods lie hidden;
They watch the heaven with eyes grown wearièd
Of hopeless dreams that come to them unbidden.

The grasshopper, from out his sandy screen,
Watching them pass redoubles his shrill song;
Dian, who loves them, makes the grass more green,

And makes the rock run water for this throng
Of ever-wandering ones whose calm eyes see
Familiar realms of darkness yet to be.

FRANCISCÆ MEÆ LAUDES

Novis te cantabo chordis,
O novelletum quod ludis
In solitudine cordis.

Esto sertis implicata,
O fœmina delicata
Per quam solvuntur peccata

Sicut beneficum Lethe,
Hauriam oscula de te,
Quæ imbuta es magnete.

Quum vitiorum tempestas
Turbabat omnes semitas,
Apparuisti, Deitas,

Velut Stella salutaris
In naufragiis amaris . . .
Suspendam cor tuis aris!

Piscina plena virtutis,
Fons æternæ juventutis,
Labris vocem redde mutis!

Quod erat spurcum, cremasti;
Quod rudius, exæquasti;
Quod debile, confirmasti!

In fame mea taberna,
In nocte mea lucerna,
Recte me semper guberna.

Adde nunc vires viribus,
Dulce balneum suavibus,
Unguentatum odoribus!

Meos circa lumbos mica,
O castitatis lorica,
Aqua tincta seraphica;

Patera gemmis corusca,
Panis salsus, mollis esca,
Divinum vinum, Francisca!

A LANDSCAPE

I would, when I compose my solemn verse,
Sleep near the heaven as do astrologers,
Near the high bells, and with a dreaming mind
Hear their calm hymns blown to me on the wind.

Out of my tower, with chin upon my hands,
I'll watch the singing, babbling human bands;
And see clock-towers like spars against the sky,
And heavens that bring thoughts of eternity;

And softly, through the mist, will watch the birth
Of stars in heaven and lamplight on the earth;
The threads of smoke that rise above the town;
The moon that pours her pale enchantment down.

Seasons will pass till Autumn fades the rose;
And when comes Winter with his weary snows,
I'll shut the doors and window-casements tight,
And build my faery palace in the night.

Then I will dream of blue horizons deep;
Of gardens where the marble fountains weep;
Of kisses, and of ever-singing birds—
A sinless Idyll built of innocent words.

And Trouble, knocking at my windowpane
And at my closet door, shall knock in vain;
I will not heed him with his stealthy tread,
Nor from my reverie uplift my head;

For I will plunge deep in the pleasure still
Of summoning the springtime with my will,
Drawing the sun out of my heart, and there
With burning thoughts making a summer air.

THE VOYAGE

I

The world is equal to the child's desire
Who plays with pictures by his nursery fire—
How vast the world by lamplight seems! How small
When memory's eyes look back, remembering all!

One morning we set forth with thoughts aflame,
Or heart o'erladen with desire or shame;
And cradle, to the song of surge and breeze,
Our own infinity on the finite seas.

Some flee the memory of their childhood's home;
And others flee their fatherland; and some,
Star-gazers drowned within a woman's eyes,
Flee from the tyrant Circe's witcheries;

And, lest they still be changed to beasts, take flight
For the embrasured heavens, and space, and light,
Till one by one the stains her kisses made
In biting cold and burning sunlight fade.

But the true voyagers are they who part
From all they love because a wandering heart
Drives them to fly the Fate they cannot fly;
Whose call is ever "On!" they know not why.

Their thoughts are like the clouds that veil a star;
They dream of change as warriors dream of war;
And strange wild wishes never twice the same:
Desires no mortal man can give a name.

II

We are like whirling tops and rolling balls—
For even when the sleepy nighttime falls,
Old Curiosity still thrusts us on,
Like the cruel Angel who goads forth the sun.

The end of fate fades ever through the air,
And, being nowhere, may be anywhere
Where a man runs, hope waking in his breast,
Forever like a madman, seeking rest.

Our souls are wandering ships outweariëd;
And one upon the bridge asks: "What's ahead?"
The topman's voice with an exultant sound
Cries: "Love and Glory!" then we run aground.

Each isle the pilot signals when 'tis late,
Is El Dorado, promised us by fate—
Imagination, spite of her belief,
Finds, in the light of dawn, a barren reef.

Oh the poor seeker after lands that flee!
Shall we not bind and cast into the sea
This drunken sailor whose ecstatic mood
Makes bitterer still the water's weary flood?

Such is an old tramp wandering in the mire,
Dreaming the paradise of his own desire,
Discovering cities of enchanted sleep
Where'er the light shines on a rubbish heap.

III

Strange voyagers, what tales of noble deeds
Deep in your dim sea-weary eyes one reads!

Open the casket where your memories are,
And show each jewel, fashioned from a star;

For I would travel without sail or wind,
And so, to lift the sorrow from my mind,
Let your long memories of sea-days far fled
Pass o'er my spirit like a sail outspread.

What have you seen?
              "We have seen waves and stars,
And lost sea-beaches, and known many wars,
And notwithstanding war and hope and fear,
We were as weary there as we are here.

"The lights that on the violet sea poured down,
The suns that set behind some far-off town,
Lit in our hearts the unquiet wish to fly
Deep in the glimmering distance of the sky;

"The loveliest countries that rich cities bless,
Never contained the strange wild loveliness
By fate and chance shaped from the floating cloud—
And we were always sorrowful and proud!

"Desire from joy gains strength in weightier measure.
Desire, old tree who draw'st thy sap from pleasure,
Though thy bark thickens as the years pass by,
Thine arduous branches rise towards the sky;

"And wilt thou still grow taller, tree more fair
Than the tall cypress?
              —Thus have we, with care,
"Gathered some flowers to please your eager mood,
Brothers who dream that distant things are good!

"We have seen many a jewel-glimmering throne;
And bowed to Idols when wild horns were blown
In palaces whose faery pomp and gleam
To your rich men would be a ruinous dream;

"And robes that were a madness to the eyes;
Women whose teeth and nails were stained with dyes;
Wise jugglers round whose neck the serpent winds——"

V

And then, and then what more?

VI

"O childish minds!

"Forget not that which we found everywhere,
From top to bottom of the fatal stair,
Above, beneath, around us and within,
The weary pageant of immortal sin.

"We have seen woman, stupid slave and proud,
Before her own frail, foolish beauty bowed;
And man, a greedy, cruel, lascivious fool,
Slave of the slave, a ripple in a pool;

"The martyrs groan, the headsman's merry mood;
And banquets seasoned and perfumed with blood;
Poison, that gives the tyrant's power the slip;
And nations amorous of the brutal whip;

"Many religions not unlike our own,
All in full flight for heaven's resplendent throne;
And Sanctity, seeking delight in pain,
Like a sick man of his own sickness vain;

"And mad mortality, drunk with its own power,
As foolish now as in a bygone hour,
Shouting, in presence of the tortured Christ:
'I curse thee, mine own Image sacrificed.'

"And silly monks in love with Lunacy,
Fleeing the troops herded by destiny,
Who seek for peace in opiate slumber furled—
Such is the pageant of the rolling world!"

VII

O bitter knowledge that the wanderers gain!
The world says our own age is little and vain;
Forever, yesterday, today, tomorrow,
'Tis horror's oasis in the sands of sorrow.

Must we depart? If you can rest, remain;
Part, if you must. Some fly, some cower in vain,
Hoping that Time, the grim and eager foe,
Will pass them by; and some run to and fro

Like the Apostles or the Wandering Jew;
Go where they will, the Slayer goes there too!
And there are some, and these are of the wise,
Who die as soon as birth has lit their eyes.

But when at length the Slayer treads us low,
We will have hope and cry, "'Tis time to go!"
As when of old we parted for Cathay
With windblown hair and eyes upon the bay.

We will embark upon the Shadowy Sea,
Like youthful wanderers for the first time free—
Hear you the lovely and funereal voice

That sings: *O come all ye whose wandering joys*
Are set upon the scented Lotus flower,
For here we sell the fruit's miraculous boon;
Come ye and drink the sweet and sleepy power
Of the enchanted, endless afternoon.

VIII

O Death, old Captain, it is time, put forth!
We have grown weary of the gloomy north;
Though sea and sky are black as ink, lift sail!
Our hearts are full of light and will not fail.

O pour thy sleepy poison in the cup!
The fire within the heart so burns us up
That we would wander Hell and Heaven through,
Deep in the Unknown seeking something *new!*

BENEDICTION

When, by the sovran will of Powers Eternal,
    The poet passed into this weary world,
His mother, filled with fears and doubts infernal,
    Clenching her hands towards Heaven these curses hurled.

—"Why rather did I not within me treasure
    "A knot of serpents than this thing of scorn?
"Accursed be the night of fleeting pleasure
    "Whence in my womb this chastisement was borne!

"Since thou hast chosen me to be the woman
    "Whose loathsome fruitfulness her husband shames,
"Who may not cast aside this birth inhuman,
    "As one that flings love-tokens to the flames,

"The hatred that on me thy vengeance launches
    "On this thwart creature I will pour in flood:
"So twist the sapling that its withered branches
    "Shall never once put forth a cankered bud!"

Regorging thus the venom of her malice,
    And misconceiving thy decrees sublime,
In deep Gehenna's gulf she fills the chalice
    Of torments destined to maternal crime.

Yet, safely sheltered by his viewless angel,
    The Childe forsaken revels in the Sun;
And all his food and drink is an evangel
    Of nectared sweets, sent by the Heavenly One.

He communes with the clouds, knows the wind's voices,
    And on his pilgrimage enchanted sings;
Seeing how like the wild bird he rejoices
    The hovering Spirit weeps and folds his wings.

All those he fain would love shrink back in terror,
    Or, boldened by his fearlessness elate,
Seek to seduce him into sin and error,
    And flesh on him the fierceness of their hate.

In bread and wine, wherewith his soul is nourished,
    They mix their ashes and foul spume impure;
Lying they cast aside the things he cherished,
    And curse the chance that made his steps their lure.

His spouse goes crying in the public places:
    "Since he doth choose my beauty to adore,
"Aping those ancient idols Time defaces
    "I would regild my glory as of yore.

"Nard, balm and myrrh shall tempt till he desires me
  "With blandishments, with dainties and with wine,
"Laughing if in a heart that so admires me
  "I may usurp the sovranty divine!

"Until aweary of love's impious orgies,
  "Fastening on him my fingers firm and frail,
"These claws, keen as the harpy's when she gorges,
  "Shall in the secret of his heart prevail.

"Then, thrilled and trembling like a young bird captured,
  "The bleeding heart shall from his breast be torn;
"To glut his maw my wanton hound, enraptured,
  "Shall see me fling it to the earth in scorn."

Heavenward, where he beholds a throne resplendent,
  The poet lifts his hands, devout and proud,
And the vast lightnings of a soul transcendent
  Veil from his gaze awhile the furious crowd:

"Blessèd be thou, my God, that givest sorrow,
  "Sole remedy divine for things unclean,
"Whence souls robust a healing virtue borrow,
  "That tempers them for sacred joys serene!

"I know thou hast ordained in blissful regions
  "A place, a welcome in the festal bowers,
"To call the poet with thy holy Legions,
  "Thrones, Dominations, Princedoms, Virtues, Powers.

"I know that Sorrow is the strength of Heaven,
  "'Gainst which in vain strive ravenous Earth and Hell,
"And that his crown must be of mysteries woven
  "Whereof all worlds and ages hold the spell.

"But not antique Palmyra's buried treasure,
 "Pearls of the sea, rare metal, precious gem,
"Though set by thine own hand could fill the measure
 "Of beauty for his radiant diadem;

"For this thy light alone, intense and tender,
 "Flows from the primal source of effluence pure,
"Whereof all mortal eyes, though bright their splendour,
 "Are but the broken glass and glimpse obscure."

ILL LUCK

To bear so vast a load of grief
 Thy courage, Sisyphus, I crave!
 My heart against the task is brave,
But Art is long and Time is brief.

Far from Fame's proud sepulchral arches,
 Towards a graveyard lone and dumb,
 My sad heart, like a muffled drum,
Goes beating slow funereal marches.

—Full many a shrouded jewel sleeps
In dark oblivion, lost in deeps
 Unknown to pick or plummet's sound:

Full many a weeping blossom flings
Her perfume, sweet as secret things,
 In silent solitudes profound.

BEAUTY

My face is a marmoreal dream, O mortals!
 And on my breast all men are bruised in turn,
 So moulded that the poet's love may burn
Mute and eternal as the earth's cold portals.

Throned like a Sphinx unveiled in the blue deep,
    A heart of snow my swan-white beauty muffles;
    I hate the line that undulates and ruffles:
And never do I laugh and never weep.

The poets, prone beneath my presence towering
    With stately port of proudest obelisks,
Worship with rites austere, their days devouring;

    For I have charms to keep their love, pure disks
That make all things more beautiful and tender:
My large eyes, radiant with eternal splendour!

IDEAL LOVE

No, never can these frail ephemeral creatures,
    The withered offspring of a worthless age,
These buskined limbs, these false and painted features,
    The hunger of a heart like mine assuage.

Leave to the laureate of sickly posies
    Gavarni's hospital sylphs, a simpering choir!
Vainly I seek among those pallid roses
    One blossom that allures my red desire.

Thou with my soul's abysmal dreams be blended,
Lady Macbeth, in crime superb and splendid,
    A dream of Æschylus flowered in cold eclipse

Of Northern suns! Thou, Night, inspire my passion,
Calm child of Angelo, coiling in strange fashion
    Thy large limbs moulded for a Titan's lips!

HYMN TO BEAUTY

Be thou from Hell upsprung or Heaven descended,
 Beauty! Thy look demoniac and divine
Pours good and evil things confusedly blended,
 And therefore art thou likened unto wine.

Thine eye with dawn is filled, with twilight dwindles,
 Like winds of night thou sprinklest perfumes mild;
Thy kiss, that is a spell, the child's heart kindles,
 Thy mouth, a chalice, makes the man a child.

Fallen from the stars or risen from gulfs of error,
 Fate dogs thy glamoured garments like a slave;
With wanton hands thou scatterest joy and terror,
 And rulest over all, cold as the grave.

Thou tramplest on the dead, scornful and cruel,
 Horror coils like an amulet round thine arms,
Crime on thy superb bosom is a jewel
 That dances amorously among its charms.

The dazzled moth that flies to thee, the candle,
 Shrivels and burns, blessing thy fatal flame;
The lover that dies fawning o'er thy sandal
 Fondles his tomb and breathes the adorĕd name.

What if from Heaven or Hell thou com'st, immortal
 Beauty? O sphinx-like monster, since alone
Thine eye, thy smile, thy hand opens the portal
 Of the Infinite I love and have not known.

What if from God or Satan be the evangel?
 Thou my sole Queen! Witch of the velvet eyes!

Since with thy fragrance, rhythm and light, O Angel!
  In a less hideous world time swiftlier flies.

EXOTIC FRAGRANCE

When, with closed eyes in the warm autumn night,
  I breathe the fragrance of thy bosom bare,
  My dream unfurls a clime of loveliest air,
Drenched in the fiery sun's unclouded light.

An indolent island dowered with heaven's delight,
  Trees singular and fruits of savour rare,
  Men having sinewy frames robust and spare,
And women whose clear eyes are wondrous bright.

Led by thy fragrance to those shores I hail
  A charmëd harbour thronged with mast and sail,
Still wearied with the quivering sea's unrest;

What time the scent of the green tamarinds
  That thrills the air and fills my swelling breast
Blends with the mariners' song and the sea-winds.

XXVIII SONNET

In undulant robes with nacreous sheen impearled
  She walks as in some stately saraband;
Or like lithe snakes by sacred charmers curled
  In cadence wreathing on the slender wand.

Calm as blue wastes of sky and desert sand
That watch unmoved the sorrows of this world;
  With slow regardless sweep as on the strand
The long swell of the woven sea-waves swirled.

Her polished orbs are like a mystic gem,
 And, while this strange and symbolled being links
 The inviolate angel and the antique sphinx,

Insphered in gold, steel, light and diadem
 The splendour of a lifeless star endows
 With clear cold majesty the barren spouse.

MUSIC

Launch me, O music, whither on the soundless
  Sea my star gleams pale!
I beneath cloudy cope or rapt in boundless
  Æther set my sail;

With breast outblown, swollen by the wind that urges
  Swelling sheets, I scale
The summit of the wave whose vexed surges
  Night from me doth veil;

A labouring vessel's passions in my pulses
  Thrill the shuddering sense;
The wind that wafts, the tempest that convulses,
  O'er the gulf immense
Swing me. Anon flat calm and clearer air
  Glass my soul's despair!

THE SPIRITUAL DAWN

When on some wallowing soul the roseate East
 Dawns with the Ideal that awakes and gnaws,
 By vengeful working of mysterious laws
An angel rises in the drowsed beast.

The inaccessible blue of the soul-sphere
> To him whose grovelling dream remorse doth gall
> Yawns wide as when the gulfs of space enthral.
So, heavenly Goddess, Spirit pure and clear,

Even on the reeking ruins of vile shame
> Thy rosy vision, beautiful and bright,
> Forever floats on my enlargëd sight.

Thus sunlight blackens the pale taper-flame;
> And thus is thy victorious phantom one,
> O soul of splendour, with the immortal Sun!

THE FLAWED BELL

Bitter and sweet it is, in winter night,
> Hard by the flickering fire that smokes, to list
While far-off memories rise in sad slow flight,
> With chimes that echo singing through the mist.

O blessëd be the bell whose vigorous throat,
> In spite of age alert, with strength unspent,
Utters religiously his faithful note,
> Like an old warrior watching near the tent!

My soul, alas! Is flawed, and when despair
Would people with her songs the chill night-air
> Too oft they faint in hoarse enfeebled tones,

> As when a wounded man forgotten moans
By the red pool, beneath a heap of dead,
And dying writhes in frenzy on his bed.

LITTLE POEMS IN PROSE

TRANSLATED BY F. P. STURM

EVERY MAN HIS CHIMÆRA

Beneath a broad grey sky, upon a vast and dusty plain devoid of grass, and where not even a nettle or a thistle was to be seen, I met several men who walked bowed down to the ground.

Each one carried upon his back an enormous Chimæra as heavy as a sack of flour or coal, or as the equipment of a Roman foot-soldier.

But the monstrous beast was not a dead weight, rather she enveloped and oppressed the men with her powerful and elastic muscles, and clawed with her two vast talons at the breast of her mount. Her fabulous head reposed upon the brow of the man like one of those horrible casques by which ancient warriors hoped to add to the terrors of the enemy.

I questioned one of the men, asking him why they went so. He replied that he knew nothing, neither he nor the others, but that evidently they went somewhere, since they were urged on by an unconquerable desire to walk.

Very curiously, none of the wayfarers seemed to be irritated by the ferocious beast hanging at his neck and cleaving to his back: one had said that he considered it as a part of himself. These grave and weary faces bore witness to no despair. Beneath the splenetic cupola of the heavens, their feet trudging through the dust of an earth as desolate as the sky, they journeyed onwards with the resigned faces of men condemned to hope forever. So the train passed me and faded into the atmosphere of the horizon at the place where the planet unveils herself to the curiosity of the human eye.

During several moments I obstinately endeavoured to comprehend this mystery; but irresistible Indifference soon threw herself upon me, nor was I more heavily dejected thereby than they by their crushing Chimæras.

VENUS AND THE FOOL

How admirable the day! The vast park swoons beneath the burning eye of the sun, as youth beneath the lordship of love.

There is no rumour of the universal ecstasy of all things. The waters themselves are as though drifting into sleep. Very different from the festivals of humanity, here is a silent revel.

It seems as though an ever-waning light makes all objects glimmer more and more, as though the excited flowers burn with a desire to rival the blue of the sky by the vividness of their colours; as though the heat, making perfumes visible, drives them in vapour towards their star.

Yet, in the midst of this universal joy, I have perceived one afflicted thing.

At the feet of a colossal Venus, one of those motley fools, those willing clowns whose business it is to bring laughter upon kings when weariness or remorse possesses them, lies wrapped in his gaudy and ridiculous garments, coiffed with his cap and bells, huddled against the pedestal, and raises towards the goddess his eyes filled with tears.

And his eyes say: "I am the last and most alone of all mortals, inferior to the meanest of animals in that I am denied either love or friendship. Yet I am made, even I, for the understanding and enjoyment of immortal Beauty. O Goddess, have pity upon my sadness and my frenzy."

The implacable Venus gazed into I know not what distances with her marble eyes.

ALREADY!

A hundred times already the sun had leaped, radiant or sad-dened, from the immense cup of the sea whose rim could scarcely be seen; a hundred times it had again sunk, glittering or morose, into its mighty bath of twilight. For many days we had contem-plated the other side of the firmament, and deciphered the celestial alphabet of the antipodes. And each of the passengers sighed and complained. One had said that the approach of land only exasperated their sufferings. "When, then," they said, "shall we cease to sleep a sleep broken by the surge, troubled by a wind that snores louder than we? When shall we be able to eat at an unmoving table?"

There were those who thought of their own firesides, who regretted their sullen, faithless wives, and their noisy progeny. All so doted upon the image of the absent land, that I believe they would have eaten grass with as much enthusiasm as the beasts.

At length a coast was signalled, and on approaching we saw a magnificent and dazzling land. It seemed as though the music of life flowed therefrom in a vague murmur; and the banks, rich with all kinds of growths, breathed, for leagues around, a deli-cious odour of flowers and fruits.

Each one therefore was joyful; his evil humour left him. Quarrels were forgotten, reciprocal wrongs forgiven, the thought of duels was blotted out of the memory, and rancour fled away like smoke.

I alone was sad, inconceivably sad. Like a priest from whom one has torn his divinity, I could not, without heartbreaking bit-terness, leave this so monstrously seductive ocean, this sea so infinitely various in its terrifying simplicity, which seemed to contain in itself and represent by its joys, and attractions, and angers, and smiles, the moods and agonies and ecstasies of all souls that have lived, that live, and that shall yet live.

In saying goodbye to this incomparable beauty I felt as though I had been smitten to death; and that is why when each of my companions said: "At last!" I could only cry *"Already!"*

Here meanwhile was the land, the land with its noises, its passions, its commodities, its festivals: a land rich and magnificent, full of promises, that sent to us a mysterious perfume of rose and musk, and from whence the music of life flowed in an amorous murmuring.

THE DOUBLE CHAMBER

A chamber that is like a reverie; a chamber truly *spiritual,* where the stagnant atmosphere is lightly touched with rose and blue.

There the soul bathes itself in indolence made odorous with regret and desire. There is some sense of the twilight, of things tinged with blue and rose: a dream of delight during an eclipse. The shape of the furniture is elongated, low, languishing; one would think it endowed with the somnambulistic vitality of plants and minerals.

The tapestries speak an inarticulate language, like the flowers, the skies, the dropping suns.

There are no artistic abominations upon the walls. Compared with the pure dream, with an impression un-analyzed, definite art, positive art, is a blasphemy. Here all has the sufficing lucidity and the delicious obscurity of music.

An infinitesimal odour of the most exquisite choice, mingled with a floating humidity, swims in this atmosphere where the drowsing spirit is lulled by the sensations one feels in a hothouse.

The abundant muslin flows before the windows and the couch, and spreads out in snowy cascades. Upon the couch lies the Idol, ruler of my dreams. But why is she here? Who has brought her? What magical power has installed her upon this throne of delight and reverie? What matter—she is there; and I recognize her.

These indeed are the eyes whose flame pierces the twilight; the subtle and terrible mirrors that I recognize by their horrifying malice. They attract, they dominate, they devour the sight of whomsoever is imprudent enough to look at them. I have often studied them; these Black Stars that compel curiosity and admiration.

To what benevolent demon, then, do I owe being thus surrounded with mystery, with silence, with peace, and sweet odours? O beatitude! The thing we name life, even in its most fortunate amplitude, has nothing in common with this supreme life with which I am now acquainted, which I taste minute by minute, second by second.

Not so! Minutes are no more; seconds are no more. Time has vanished, and Eternity reigns—an Eternity of delight.

A heavy and terrible knocking reverberates upon the door, and, as in a hellish dream, it seems to me as though I had received a blow from a mattock.

Then a Spectre enters: it is an usher who comes to torture me in the name of the Law; an infamous concubine who comes to cry misery and to add the trivialities of her life to the sorrow of mine; or it may be the errand-boy of an editor who comes to implore the remainder of a manuscript.

The Chamber of paradise, the Idol, the ruler of dreams, the Sylphide, as the great René said; all this magic has vanished at the brutal knocking of the Spectre.

Horror; I remember, I remember! Yes, this kennel, this habitation of eternal weariness, is indeed my own. There is my senseless furniture, dusty and tattered; the dirty fireplace without a flame or an ember; the sad windows where the raindrops have traced runnels in the dust; the manuscripts, erased or unfinished; the almanac with the sinister days marked off with a pencil!

And this perfume of another world, whereof I intoxicated myself with a so perfected sensitiveness; alas, Its place is taken by an odour of stale tobacco smoke, mingled with I know not what nauseating mustiness. Now one breathes here the rankness of desolation.

In this narrow world, narrow and yet full of disgust, a single familiar object smiles at me: the phial of laudanum: old and terrible love; like all loves, alas! Fruitful in caresses and treacheries.

Yes, Time has reappeared; Time reigns a monarch now; and with the hideous Ancient has returned all his demoniacal following of Memories, Regrets, Tremors, Fears, Dolours, Nightmares, and twittering nerves.

I assure you that the seconds are strongly and solemnly accentuated now; and each, as it drips from the pendulum, says: "I am Life: intolerable, implacable Life!"

There is not a second in mortal life whose mission it is to bear good news: the good news that brings the inexplicable tear to the eye.

Yes, Time reigns; Time has regained his brutal mastery. And he goads me, as though I were a steer, with his double goad: "Whoa, thou fool! Sweat, then, thou slave! Live on, thou damnèd!"

AT ONE O'CLOCK IN THE MORNING

Alone at last! Nothing is to be heard but the rattle of a few tardy and tired-out cabs. There will be silence now, if not repose, for several hours at least. At last the tyranny of the human face has disappeared—I shall not suffer except alone. At last it is permitted me to refresh myself in a bath of shadows. But first a double turn of the key in the lock. It seems to me that this turn of the key will deepen my solitude and strengthen the barriers which actually separate me from the world.

A horrible life and a horrible city! Let us run over the events of the day. I have seen several literary men; one of them wished to know if he could get to Russia by land (he seemed to have an idea that Russia was an island); I have disputed generously enough with the editor of a review, who to each objection replied: "We take the part of respectable people," which implies that every other paper but his own is edited by a knave; I have saluted some twenty people, fifteen of them unknown to me; and shaken hands with a like number, without having taken the precaution of first buying gloves; I have been driven to kill time, during a shower, with a mountebank, who wanted me to design for her a costume as Venusta; I have made my bow to a theatre manager, who said: "You will do well, perhaps, to interview Z; he is the heaviest, foolishest, and most celebrated of all my authors; with him perhaps you will be able to come to something. See him, and then we'll see." I have boasted (why?) of several villainous deeds I never committed, and indignantly denied certain shameful things I accomplished with joy, certain misdeeds of fanfaronade, crimes of human respect; I have refused an easy favour to a friend and given a written recommendation to a perfect fool. Heavens! It's well ended.

Discontented with myself and with everything and everybody else, I should be glad enough to redeem myself and regain my self-respect in the silence and solitude.

Souls of those whom I have loved, whom I have sung, fortify me; sustain me; drive away the lies and the corrupting vapours of this world; and Thou, Lord my God, accord me so much grace as shall produce some beautiful verse to prove to myself that I am not the last of men, that I am not inferior to those I despise.

THE CONFITEOR OF THE ARTIST

How penetrating is the end of an autumn day! Ah, yes, penetrating enough to be painful even; for there are certain delicious sensations whose vagueness does not prevent them from being intense; and none more keen than the perception of the Infinite. He has a great delight who drowns his gaze in the immensity of sky and sea. Solitude, silence, the incomparable chastity of the azure—a little sail trembling upon the horizon, by its very littleness and isolation imitating my irremediable existence—the melodious monotone of the surge—all these things thinking through me and I through them (for in the grandeur of the reverie the Ego is swiftly lost); they think, I say, but musically and picturesquely, without quibbles, without syllogisms, without deductions.

These thoughts, as they arise in me or spring forth from external objects, soon become always too intense. The energy working within pleasure creates an uneasiness, a positive suffering. My nerves are too tense to give other than clamouring and dolorous vibrations.

And now the profundity of the sky dismays me; its limpidity exasperates me. The insensibility of the sea, the immutability of the spectacle, revolt me. Ah, must one eternally suffer, forever be a fugitive from Beauty?

Nature, pitiless enchantress, ever-victorious rival, leave me! Tempt my desires and my pride no more. The contemplation of Beauty is a duel where the artist screams with terror before being vanquished.

THE THYRSUS

TO FRANZ LISZT

What is a thyrsus? According to the moral and poetical sense, it is a sacerdotal emblem in the hand of the priests or priestesses celebrating the divinity of whom they are the interpreters and servants. But physically it is no more than a baton, a pure staff, a hop-pole, a vine-prop; dry, straight, and hard. Around this baton, in capricious meanderings, stems and flowers twine and wanton; these, sinuous and fugitive; those, hanging like bells or inverted cups. And an astonishing complexity disengages itself from this complexity of tender or brilliant lines and colours. Would not one suppose that the curved line and the spiral pay their court to the straight line, and twine about in a mute adoration? Would not one say that all these delicate corollæ, all these calices, explosions of odours and colours, execute a mystical dance around the hieratic staff? And what imprudent mortal will dare to decide whether the flowers and the vine branches have been made for the baton, or whether the baton is not but a pretext to set forth the beauty of the vine branches and the flowers?

The thyrsus is the symbol of your astonishing duality, O powerful and venerated master, dear bacchanal of a mysterious and impassioned Beauty. Never a nymph excited by the mysterious Dionysius shook her thyrsus over the heads of her companions with as much energy as your genius trembles in the hearts of your brothers. The baton is your will: erect, firm, unshakeable; the flowers are the wanderings of your fancy around it: the feminine element encircling the masculine with her illusive dance. Straight line and arabesque—intention and expression—the rigidity of the will and the suppleness of the word—a variety of means united for a single purpose—the all-powerful and indivisible amalgam that is genius—what analyst will have the detestable courage to divide or to separate you?

Dear Liszt, across the fogs, beyond the flowers, in towns where the pianos chant your glory, where the printing-house translates your wisdom; in whatever place you be, in the splendour of the Eternal City or among the fogs of the dreamy towns that Cambrinus consoles; improvising rituals of delight or ineffable pain, or giving to paper your abstruse meditations; singer of eternal pleasure and pain, philosopher, poet, and artist, I offer you the salutation of immortality!

THE MARKSMAN

As the carriage traversed the wood he bade the driver draw up in the neighbourhood of a shooting gallery, saying that he would like to have a few shots to kill time. Is not the slaying of the monster

Time the most ordinary and legitimate occupation of man? So he gallantly offered his hand to his dear, adorable, and execrable wife; the mysterious woman to whom he owed so many pleasures, so many pains, and perhaps also a great part of his genius.

Several bullets went wide of the proposed mark, one of them flew far into the heavens, and as the charming creature laughed deliriously, mocking the clumsiness of her husband, he turned to her brusquely and said: "Observe that doll yonder, to the right, with its nose in the air, and with so haughty an appearance. Very well, dear angel, *I will imagine to myself that it is you!*"

He closed both eyes and pulled the trigger. The doll was neatly decapitated.

Then, bending towards his dear, adorable, and execrable wife, his inevitable and pitiless muse, he kissed her respectfully upon the hand, and added, "Ah, dear angel, how I thank you for my skill!"

THE SHOOTING-RANGE AND THE CEMETERY

"Cemetery View Inn"—"A queer sign," said our traveller to himself; "but it raises a thirst! Certainly the keeper of this inn appreciates Horace and the poet pupils of Epicurus. Perhaps he even apprehends the profound philosophy of those old Egyptians who had no feast without its skeleton, or some emblem of life's brevity."

He entered: drank a glass of beer in presence of the tombs; and slowly smoked a cigar. Then, his phantasy driving him, he went down into the cemetery, where the grass was so tall and inviting; so brilliant in the sunshine.

The light and heat, indeed, were so furiously intense that one had said the drunken sun wallowed upon a carpet of flowers that had fattened upon the corruption beneath.

The air was heavy with vivid rumours of life—the life of things infinitely small—and broken at intervals by the crackling of shots from a neighbouring shooting-range, that exploded with a sound as of champagne corks to the burden of a hollow symphony.

And then, beneath a sun which scorched the brain, and in that atmosphere charged with the ardent perfume of death, he heard a voice whispering out of the tomb where he sat. And this voice said: "Accursed be your rifles and targets, you turbulent living ones, who care so little for the dead in their divine repose! Accursed be your ambitions and calculations, importunate mortals who study the arts of slaughter near the sanctuary of Death himself! Did you but know how easy the prize to win, how facile the end to reach, and how all save Death is naught, not so greatly would you fatigue yourselves, O ye laborious alive; nor would you so often vex the slumber of them that long ago reached the End—the only true end of life detestable!"

THE DESIRE TO PAINT

Unhappy perhaps is the man, but happy the artist, who is torn with this desire.

I burn to paint a certain woman who has appeared to me so rarely, and so swiftly fled away, like some beautiful, regrettable thing the traveller must leave behind him in the night. It is already long since I saw her.

She is beautiful, and more than beautiful: she is overpowering. The colour black preponderates in her; all that she inspires is nocturnal and profound. Her eyes are two caverns where mystery vaguely stirs and gleams; her glance illuminates like a ray of light; it is an explosion in the darkness.

I would compare her to a black sun if one could conceive of a dark star overthrowing light and happiness. But it is the moon that she makes one dream of most readily; the moon, who has without doubt touched her with her own influence; not the white moon of the idylls, who resembles a cold bride, but the sinister and intoxicating moon suspended in the depths of a stormy night, among the driven clouds; not the discreet peaceful moon who visits the dreams of pure men, but the moon torn from the sky, conquered and revolted, that the witches of Thessaly hardly constrain to dance upon the terrified grass.

Her small brow is the habitation of a tenacious will and the love of prey. And below this inquiet face, whose mobile nostrils breathe in the unknown and the impossible, glitters, with an unspeakable grace, the smile of a large mouth; white, red, and delicious; a mouth that makes one dream of the miracle of some superb flower unclosing in a volcanic land.

There are women who inspire one with the desire to woo them and win them; but she makes one wish to die slowly beneath her steady gaze.

THE GLASS-VENDOR

There are some natures purely contemplative and antipathetic to action, who nevertheless, under a mysterious and inexplicable impulse, sometimes act with a rapidity of which they would have believed themselves incapable. Such a one is he who, fearing to find some new vexation awaiting him at his lodgings, prowls about in a cowardly fashion before the door without daring to enter; such a one is he who keeps a letter fifteen days without opening it, or only makes up his mind at the end of six months to undertake a journey that has been a necessity for a year past. Such beings sometimes feel themselves precipitately thrust towards action, like an arrow from a bow.

The novelist and the physician, who profess to know all things, yet cannot explain whence comes this sudden and delirious energy to indolent and voluptuous souls; nor how, incapable of accomplishing the simplest and most necessary things, they are at some certain moment of time possessed by a superabundant hardihood which enables them to execute the most absurd and even the most dangerous acts.

One of my friends, the most harmless dreamer that ever lived, at one time set fire to a forest, in order to ascertain, as he said, whether the flames take hold with the easiness that is commonly affirmed. His experiment failed ten times running, on the eleventh it succeeded only too well.

Another lit a cigar by the side of a powder barrel, *in order to see, to know, to tempt Destiny,* for a jest, to have the pleasure of suspense, for no reason at all, out of caprice, out of idleness. This is a kind of energy that springs from weariness and reverie; and those in whom it manifests so stubbornly are in general, as I have said, the most indolent and dreamy beings.

Another so timid that he must cast down his eyes before the gaze of any man, and summon all his poor will before he dare enter a café or pass the pay-box of a theatre, where the ticket-seller seems, in his eyes, invested with all the majesty of Minos, Æcus, and Rhadamanthus, will at times throw himself upon the neck of some old man whom he sees in the street, and embrace him with enthusiasm in sight of an astonished crowd. Why? Because—because this countenance is irresistibly attractive to him? Perhaps; but it is more legitimate to suppose that he himself does not know why.

I have been more than once a victim to these crises and outbreaks which give us cause to believe that evil-meaning demons slip into us, to make us the ignorant accomplices of their most absurd desires. One morning I arose in a sullen mood, very sad, and tired of idleness, and thrust as it seemed to me to the doing of some great thing, some brilliant act—and then, alas, I opened the window.

(I beg you to observe that in some people the spirit of mystification is not the result of labour or combination, but rather of a fortuitous inspiration which would partake, were it not for the strength of the feeling, of the mood called hysterical by the physician and satanic by those who think a little more profoundly than the physician; the mood which thrusts us unresisting to a multitude of dangerous and inconvenient acts.)

The first person I noticed in the street was a glass-vendor whose shrill and discordant cry mounted up to me through the heavy, dull atmosphere of Paris. It would have been else impossible to account for the sudden and despotic hatred of this poor man that came upon me.

"Hello, there!" I cried, and bade him ascend. Meanwhile I reflected, not without gaiety, that as my room was on the sixth landing, and the stairway very narrow, the man would have some difficulty in ascending, and in many a place would break off the corners of his fragile merchandise.

At length he appeared. I examined all his glasses with curiosity, and then said to him: "What, have you no coloured glasses? Glasses of rose and crimson and blue, magical glasses, glasses of Paradise? You are insolent. You dare to walk in mean streets when you have no glasses that would make one see beauty in life?" And I hurried him briskly to the staircase, which he staggered down, grumbling.

I went on to the balcony and caught up a little flowerpot, and when the man appeared in the doorway beneath I let fall my engine of war perpendicularly upon the edge of his pack, so that it was upset by the shock and all his poor walking fortune broken to bits. It made a noise like a palace of crystal shattered by lightning. Mad with my folly, I cried furiously after him: "The life beautiful! The life beautiful!"

Such nervous pleasantries are not without peril; often enough one pays dearly for them. But what matters an eternity of damnation to him who has found in one second an eternity of enjoyment?

THE WIDOWS

Vauvenargues says that in public gardens there are alleys haunted principally by thwarted ambition, by unfortunate inventors, by aborted glories and broken hearts, and by all those tumultuous and contracted souls in whom the last sighs of the storm mutter yet again, and who thus betake themselves far from the insolent and joyous eyes of the well-to-do. These shadowy retreats are the rendezvous of life's cripples.

To such places above all others do the poet and philosopher direct their avid conjectures. They find there an unfailing pasturage, for if there is one place they disdain to visit it is, as I have already hinted, the place of the joy of the rich. A turmoil in the void has no attractions for them. On the contrary, they feel themselves irresistibly drawn towards all that is feeble, ruined, sorrowing, and bereft.

An experienced eye is never deceived. In these rigid and dejected lineaments; in these eyes, wan and hollow, or bright with the last fading gleams of the combat against fate; in these numerous profound wrinkles and in the slow and troubled gait, the eye of experience deciphers unnumbered legends of mistaken devotion, of unrewarded effort, of hunger and cold humbly and silently supported.

Have you not at times seen widows sitting on the deserted benches? Poor widows, I mean. Whether in mourning or not they are easily recognised. Moreover, there is always something wanting in the mourning of the poor; a lack of harmony which but renders it the more heartbreaking. It is forced to be niggardly in its show of grief. They are the rich who exhibit a full complement of sorrow.

Who is the saddest and most saddening of widows: she who leads by the hand a child who cannot share her reveries, or she who is quite alone? I do not know. . . . It happened that I once followed for several long hours an aged and afflicted woman of this kind: rigid and erect, wrapped in a little worn shawl, she carried in all her being the pride of stoicism.

She was evidently condemned by her absolute loneliness to the habits of an ancient celibacy; and the masculine characters of her habits added to their austerity a piquant mysteriousness. In what miserable café she dines I know not, nor in what manner. I followed her to a reading-room, and for a long time watched her reading the papers, her active eyes, that once burned with tears, seeking for news of a powerful and personal interest.

At length, in the afternoon, under a charming autumnal sky, one of those skies that let fall hosts of memories and regrets, she seated herself remotely in a garden, to listen, far from the crowd, to one of the regimental bands whose music gratifies the people of Paris. This was without doubt the small debauch of the innocent old woman (or the purified old woman), the well-earned consolation for another of the burdensome days without a friend, without conversation, without joy, without a confidant, that God had allowed to fall upon her perhaps for many years past—three hundred and sixty-five times a year!

Yet one more:

I can never prevent myself from throwing a glance, if not sympathetic at least full of curiosity, over the crowd of outcasts who press around the enclosure of a public concert. From the orchestra, across the night, float songs of fête, of triumph, or of pleasure. The dresses of the women sweep and shimmer; glances pass; the well-to-do, tired with doing nothing, saunter about and make indolent pretence of listening to the music. Here are only the rich, the happy; here is nothing that does not inspire or exhale the pleasure of being alive, except the aspect of the mob that presses against the outer barrier yonder, catching gratis, at the will of the wind, a tatter of music, and watching the glittering furnace within.

There is a reflection of the joy of the rich deep in the eyes of the poor that is always interesting. But today, beyond this people dressed in blouses and calico, I saw one whose nobility was in striking contrast with all the surrounding triviality. She was a tall, majestic woman, and so imperious in all her air that I cannot remember having seen the like in the collections of the aristo-cratic beauties of the past. A perfume of exalted virtue emanated from all her being. Her face, sad and worn, was in perfect keep-ing with the deep mourning in which she was dressed. She also, like the plebeians she mingled with and did not see, looked upon the luminous world with a profound eye, and listened with a toss of her head.

It was a strange vision. "Most certainly," I said to myself, "this poverty, if poverty it be, ought not to admit of any sordid econ-omy; so noble a face answers for that. Why then does she remain in surroundings with which she is so strikingly in contrast?"

But in curiously passing near her I was able to divine the rea-son. The tall widow held by the hand a child dressed like herself in black. Modest as was the price of entry, this price perhaps sufficed to pay for some of the needs of the little being, or even more, for a superfluity, a toy.

She will return on foot, dreaming and meditating—and alone, always alone, for the child is turbulent and selfish, without gen-tleness or patience, and cannot become, anymore than another animal, a dog or a cat, the confidant of solitary griefs.

THE TEMPTATIONS; OR, EROS, PLUTUS, AND GLORY

Last night two superb Satans and a She-devil not less extraordi-nary ascended the mysterious stairway by which Hell gains access to the frailty of sleeping man, and communes with him in secret. These three postured gloriously before me, as though they had been upon a stage—and a sulphurous splendour ema-nated from these beings who so disengaged themselves from the opaque heart of the night. They bore with them so proud a pres-ence, and so full of mastery, that at first I took them for three of the true Gods.

The first Satan, by his face, was a creature of doubtful sex. The softness of an ancient Bacchus shone in the lines of his body. His beautiful languorous eyes, of a tenebrous and indefinite colour, were like violets still laden with the heavy tears of the storm; his slightly parted lips were like heated censers, from whence exhaled the sweet savour of many perfumes; and each time he breathed, exotic insects drew, as they fluttered, strength from the ardours of his breath.

Twined about his tunic of purple stuff, in the manner of a cincture, was an iridescent Serpent with lifted head and eyes like embers turned sleepily towards him. Phials full of sinister fluids, alternating with shining knives and instruments of surgery, hung from this living girdle. He held in his right hand a flagon containing a luminous red fluid, and inscribed with a legend in these singular words:

DRINK OF THIS MY BLOOD: A PERFECT RESTORATIVE;

and in his left hand held a violin that without doubt served to sing his pleasures and pains, and to spread abroad the contagion of his folly upon the nights of the Sabbath.

From rings upon his delicate ankles trailed a broken chain of gold, and when the burden of this caused him to bend his eyes towards the earth, he would contemplate with vanity the nails of his feet, as brilliant and polished as well-wrought jewels.

He looked at me with eyes inconsolably heartbroken and giving forth an insidious intoxication, and cried in a chanting voice: "If thou wilt, if thou wilt, I will make thee an overlord of souls; thou shalt be master of living matter more perfectly than the sculptor is master of his clay; thou shalt taste the pleasure, reborn without end, of obliterating thyself in the self of another, and of luring other souls to lose themselves in thine."

But I replied to him: "I thank thee. I only gain from this venture, then, beings of no more worth than my poor self? Though remembrance brings me shame indeed, I would forget nothing;

and even before I recognised thee, thou ancient monster, thy mysterious cutlery, thy equivocal phials, and the chain that imprisons thy feet, were symbols showing clearly enough the inconvenience of thy friendship. Keep thy gifts."

The second Satan had neither the air at once tragical and smiling, the lovely insinuating ways, nor the delicate and scented beauty of the first. A gigantic man, with a coarse, eyeless face, his heavy paunch overhung his hips and was gilded and pictured, like a tattooing, with a crowd of little moving figures which represented the unnumbered forms of universal misery. There were little sinew-shrunken men who hung themselves willingly from nails; there were meagre gnomes, deformed and undersized, whose beseeching eyes begged an alms even more eloquently than their trembling hands; there were old mothers who nursed clinging abortions at their pendent breasts. And many others, even more surprising.

This heavy Satan beat with his fist upon his immense belly, from whence came a loud and resounding metallic clangour, which died away in a sighing made by many human voices. And he smiled unrestrainedly, showing his broken teeth—the imbecile smile of a man who has dined too freely. Then the creature said to me:

"I can give thee that which gets all, which is worth all, which takes the place of all." And he tapped his monstrous paunch, whence came a sonorous echo as the commentary to his obscene speech. I turned away with disgust and replied: "I need no man's misery to bring me happiness; nor will I have the sad wealth of all the misfortunes pictured upon thy skin as upon a tapestry."

As for the She-devil, I should lie if I denied that at first I found in her a certain strange charm, which to define I can but compare to the charm of certain beautiful women past their first youth, who yet seem to age no more, whose beauty keeps something of the penetrating magic of ruins. She had an air at once imperious and sordid, and her eyes, though heavy, held a certain power of fascination. I was struck most by her voice, wherein I found the remembrance of the most delicious *contralti,* as well as a little of the hoarseness of a throat continually laved with brandy.

"Wouldst thou know my power?" said the charming and paradoxical voice of the false goddess. "Then listen." And she put to her mouth a gigantic trumpet, enribboned, like a *mirliton,* with the titles of all the newspapers in the world; and through this trumpet she cried my name so that it rolled through space with the sound of a hundred thousand thunders, and came reechoing back to me from the farthest planet.

"Devil!" cried I, half tempted. "That at least is worth something." But it vaguely struck me, upon examining the seductive virago more attentively, that I had seen her clinking glasses with certain drolls of my acquaintance, and her blare of brass carried to my ears I know not what memory of a fanfare prostituted.

So I replied, with all disdain: "Get thee hence! I know better than wed the light o' love of them that I will not name."

Truly, I had the right to be proud of a so courageous renunciation. But unfortunately I awoke, and all my courage left me. "In truth," I said, "I must have been very deeply asleep indeed to have had such scruples. Ah, if they would but return while I am awake, I would not be so delicate."

So I invoked the three in a loud voice, offering to dishonour myself as often as necessary to obtain their favours; but I had without doubt too deeply offended them, for they have never returned.

POEMS IN PROSE

TRANSLATED BY JOSEPH T. SHIPLEY

DEDICATION TO ARSÈNE HOUSSAYE

MY DEAR FRIEND:

I send you a little work of which it cannot be said, without injustice, that it has neither head nor tail; since all of it, on the contrary, is at once head and tail, alternately and reciprocally. Consider, I pray you, what convenience this arrangement offers to all of us, to you, to me and to the reader. We can stop where we wish, I my musing, you your consideration, and the reader his perusal—for I do not hold the latter's restive will by the interminable thread of a fine-spun intrigue. Remove a vertebra, and the two parts of this tortuous fantasy rejoin painlessly. Chop it into particles, and you will see that each part can exist by itself. In the hope that some of these segments will be lively enough to please and to amuse you, I venture to dedicate to you the entire serpent.

I have a little confession to make. It was while glancing, for at least the twentieth time, through the famous *Gaspard de la Nuit,* by Aloysius Bertrand (a book known to you, to me, and to a few of our friends, has it not the highest right to be called famous?), that the idea came to me to attempt an analogous plan, and to apply to the description of modern life, or rather of *a* life modern and more abstract, the process which he applied in the depicting of ancient life, so strangely picturesque.

Which of us has not, in his moments of ambition, dreamed the miracle of a poetic prose, musical without rhythm or rime, sufficiently supple, sufficiently abrupt, to adapt itself to the lyrical movements of the soul, to the windings and turnings of the fancy, to the sudden starts of the conscience?

It is particularly in frequenting great cities, it is from the flux of their innumerable streams of intercourse, that this importunate ideal is born. Have not you yourself, my dear friend, tried to convey in a chanson the strident cry of the glazier, and to express in a lyric prose all the grievous suggestions that cry bears even to the housetops, through the heaviest mists of the street?

But, to speak truth, I fear that my jealousy has not brought me good fortune. As soon as I had begun the work, I saw that not only was I laboring far, far, from my mysterious and brilliant model, but that I was reaching an accomplishment (if it can be called *an accomplishment*) peculiarly different—accident of which all others would doubtless be proud, but which can but profoundly humiliate a mind which considers it the highest honor of the poet to achieve exactly what he has planned.

Devotedly yours,

C. B.

A JESTER

It was the outburst of the New Year: chaos of mud and snow, crossed by a thousand coaches, sparkling with baubles and gew-gaws, swarming with desires and with despairs, official folly of a great city made to weaken the fortitude of the firmest eremite.

In the midst of this hubbub and tumult, a donkey was trotting along, tormented by a lout with a horsewhip.

As the donkey was about to turn a corner, a fine fellow, gloved, polished, with a merciless cravat, and imprisoned in impeccable garments, bowed ceremoniously before the beast; said to it, removing his hat: "I greet thee, good and happy one"; and turned towards some companions with a fatuous air, as though requesting them to add their approbation to his content.

The donkey did not see the clever jester, and continued steadily where its duty called.

As for me, I was overcome by an inordinate rage against the sublime idiot, who seemed to me to concentrate in himself the wit of France.

THE DOG AND THE VIAL

"My pretty dog, my good dog, my doggy dear, come and smell this excellent perfume bought at the best scent-shop in the city."

And the dog, wagging its tail, which is, I think, the poor creature's substitute for a laugh or a smile, approached and curiously placed its damp nose to the opened vial; then, recoiling with sudden fright, it growled at me in reproach.

"Ah! Wretched dog, if I had offered you a mass of excrement, you would have smelled it with delight, and probably have devoured it. So even you, unworthy companion of my unhappy life, resemble the public, to whom one must never offer delicate perfumes, which exasperate, but carefully raked-up mire."

THE WILD WOMAN AND THE COQUETTE

"Really, my dear, you tire me immeasurably and unpityingly; one would say, to hear you sigh, that you suffered more than the sexagenarian gleaners or the old beggar hags who pick up crusts at the doors of restaurants.

"If at least your sighs expressed remorse, they would do you some honor; but they convey merely the surfeit of well-being and the languor of repose. And, too, you will not stop your constant flow of needless words: 'Love me well! I have so much need! Comfort me thus, caress me so!'

"Come! I shall try to cure you; perhaps we shall find a means, for two cents, in the midst of a fair, not far away.

"Take a good look, I pray you, at this strong iron cage, within which moves, howling like a damned soul, shaking the bars like an ourang-outang enraged by exile, imitating to perfection, now the circular bounds of the tiger, now the clumsy waddling of the polar bear, that hairy monster whose form vaguely resembles your own.

"That monster is one of those beasts one usually calls 'my angel'—that is, a woman. The other monster, he who bawls at the top of his voice, club in his hand, is a husband. He has chained his lawful wife like a beast, and he exhibits her in the suburbs on fair days—with the magistrates' permission, of course.

"Pay close attention. See with what voracity (perhaps not feigned) she tears apart the living rabbits and the cackling fowl her keeper throws her. 'Come,' he says, 'one must not eat one's whole store in a day'; and, with that wise word, he cruelly snatches the prey, the winding entrails of which remain a moment caught on the teeth of the ferocious beast—I mean, the woman.

"Come! A good blow to calm her! For she darts terrible glances of lust at the stolen food. Good God! The club is not a jester's slap stick! Did you hear the flesh resound, right through the artificial hair? Her eyes leap from her head now; she howls *more naturally*. In her rage she sparkles all over, like smitten iron.

"Such are the conjugal customs of these two children of Adam and Eve, these works of Thy hands, O my God! This woman is doubtless miserable, though after all, perhaps, the titillating joys of glory are not unknown to her. There are misfortunes less remediable, and with no compensation. But in the world to which she has been thrown, she has never been able to think that woman might deserve a different destiny.

"Now, as for us two, my fine lady! Seeing the hells of which the world is made, what would you have me think of your pretty hell, you who rest only on stuffs as soft as your own skin, who eat only cooked viands, for whom a skilled domestic takes care to cut the bites?

"And what can mean to me all these soft signs which heave your perfumed breast, my lusty coquette? And all those affectations learned from books, and that everlasting melancholy, intended to arouse an emotion far other than pity? Indeed, I sometimes feel like teaching you what true misfortune means.

"Seeing you so, my beautiful dainty one, your feet in the mire and your moist eyes turned to the sky, as though to demand a king, one would say indeed: a young frog invoking the ideal. If you scorn the log (which I am now, you know), beware the stork which will *kill, swallow, devour you* at its caprice.

"Poet as I am, I am not such a fool as you may think, and if you tire me too often with your whining affectations, I shall treat you as a wild woman, or throw you through the window as an empty flask."

THE OLD MOUNTEBANK

Everywhere the holiday crowd was parading, spread out, merry making. It was one of those festivals on which mountebanks, tricksters, animal trainers and itinerant merchants had long been relying, to compensate for the dull seasons of the year.

On such days it seems to me the people forget all, sadness and work; they become children. For the little ones, it is a day of leave, the horror of the school put off twenty-four hours. For the grown-ups, it is an armistice, concluded with the malevolent forces of life, a respite in the universal contention and struggle.

The man of the world himself, and even he who is occupied with spiritual tasks, with difficulty escape the influence of this popular jubilee. They absorb, without volition, their part of the atmosphere of devil-may-care. As for me, I never fail, like a true Parisian, to inspect all the booths that flaunt themselves in these solemn epochæ.

They made, in truth, a formidable gathering: they bawled, bellowed, howled. It was a mingling of cries, of blaring of brass and bursting of rockets. The clowns and the simpletons convulsed the features of their swarthy faces, hardened by wind, rain, and sun; they hurled forth, with the assurance of comedians certain of their wares, witticisms and pleasantries of a humor solid and heavy as that of Molière. The Hercules, proud of the enormousness of their limbs, without forehead, without cranium, stalked majestically about under fleshings fresh washed for the occasion. The dancers, pretty as fairies or as princesses, leapt and cavorted under the flare of lanterns which filled their skirts with sparkles.

All was light, dust, shouting, joy, tumult; some spent, others gained, the one and the other equally joyful. Children clung to their mothers' skirts to obtain a sugar-stick, or climbed upon their fathers' shoulders the better to see a conjurer dazzling as a god. And spread over all, dominating every odor, was a smell of frying, which was the incense of the festival.

At the end, at the extreme end of the row of booths, as if, ashamed, he had exiled himself from all these splendors, I saw an old mountebank, stooped, decrepit, emaciated, a ruin of a man, leaning against one of the pillars of his hut, more wretched than that of the most besotted barbarian, the distress of which two candle ends, guttering and smoking, lighted up only too well.

Everywhere was joy, gain, revelry; everywhere certainty of the morrow's bread; everywhere the frenetic outbursts of vitality. Here, absolute misery, misery bedecked, to crown the horror, in comic tatters, where necessity, rather than art, produced the contrast. He was not laughing, the wretched one! He was not weeping, he was not dancing, he was not gesticulating, he was not crying. He was singing no song, gay or grievous, he was imploring no one. He was mute and immobile. He had renounced, he had withdrawn. His destiny was accomplished.

But what a deep, unforgettable look he cast over the crowd and the lights, the moving stream of which was stemmed a few yards from his repulsive wretchedness! I felt my throat clutched by the terrible hand of hysteria, and it seemed as though glances were clouded by rebellious tears that would not fall.

What was to be done? What good was there in asking the unfortunate what curiosity, what marvel had he to show within those barefaced shades, behind that threadbare curtain? In truth, I dared not; and, although the reason for my timidity will make you laugh, I confess that I was afraid of humiliating him. At length, I had resolved to drop a coin while passing his boards, in the hope that he would divine my purpose, when a great backwash of people, produced by I know not what disturbance, carried me far away.

And leaving, obsessed by the sight, I sought to analyze my sudden sadness, and I said: "I have just seen the image of the aged man of letters, who has survived the generation of which he was the brilliant entertainer; of the old poet, friendless, without family, without child, degraded by his misery and by public ingratitude, into whose booth a forgetful world no longer wants to go!"

THE CLOCK

The Chinese tell the time in the eyes of cats. One day a missionary, walking in the suburbs of Nanking, noticed that he had forgotten his watch, and asked a little boy what time it was.

The youngster of the heavenly Empire hesitated at first; then, carried away by his thought he answered: "I'll tell you." A few moments later he reappeared, bearing in his arms an immense cat, and looking, as they say, into the whites of its eyes, he announced without hesitation: "It's not quite noon." Which was the fact.

As for me, if I turn toward the fair feline, to her so aptly named, who is at once the honor of her sex, the pride of my heart and the fragrance of my mind, be it by night or by day, in the full light or in the opaque shadows, in the depths of her adorable eyes I always tell the time distinctly, always the same, a vast, a solemn, hour, large as space, without division of minutes or of seconds—an immovable hour which is not marked on the clocks, yet is slight as a sigh, is rapid as the lifting of a lash.

And if some intruder comes to disturb me while my glance rests upon that charming dial, if some rude and intolerant genie, some demon of the evil hour, comes to ask: "What are you looking at so carefully? What are you hunting for in the eyes of that being? Do you see the time there, mortal squanderer and do-nothing?" I shall answer, unhesitant: "Yes, I see the time, it is Eternity!"

Is not this, madame, a really worthwhile madrigal, just as affected as yourself? Indeed, I have had so much pleasure in embroidering this pretentious gallantry, that I shall ask you for nothing in exchange.

A HEMISPHERE IN A TRESS

Let me breathe, long, long, of the odor of your hair, let me plunge my whole face in its depth, as a thirsty man in the waters of a spring, let me flutter it with my hand as a perfumed kerchief, to shake off memories into the air.

If you could know all that I see! All that I feel! All that I understand in your hair! My soul journeys on perfumes as the souls of other men on music.

Your hair meshes a full dream, crowded with sails and masts; it holds great seas on which monsoons bear me toward charming climes, where the skies are bluer and deeper, where the atmosphere is perfumed with fruits, with leaves, and with the human skin.

In the ocean of your hair I behold a port humming with melancholy chants, with strong men of all nations and with ships of every form carving their delicate, intricate architecture on an enormous sky where lolls eternal heat.

In the caresses of your hair, I find again the languor of long hours on a divan, in the cabin of a goodly ship, cradled by the unnoticed undulation of the port, between pots of flowers and refreshing water-jugs.

At the glowing hearthstone of your hair, I breathe the odor of tobacco mixed with opium and sugar; in the night of your hair, I see shine forth the infinite of the tropic sky; on the downy banksides of your hair, I grow drunk with the mingled odors of tar and musk, and oil of cocoanut.

Let me bite, long, your thick black hair. When I nibble your springy, rebellious hair, it seems that I am eating memories.

THE PLAYTHING OF THE POOR

I should like to give you an idea for an innocent diversion. There are so few amusements that are not guilty ones!

When you go out in the morning for a stroll along the highways, fill your pockets with little penny contrivances—such as the straight merryandrew moved by a single thread, the blacksmiths who strike the anvil, the rider and his horse, with a whistle for a tail—and, along the taverns, at the foot of the trees, make presents of them to the unknown poor children whom you meet. You will see their eyes grow beyond all measure. At first, they will not dare to take; they will doubt their good fortune. Then their hands will eagerly seize the gift, and they will flee as do the cats who go far off to eat the bit you have given them, having learned to distrust man.

On a road, behind the rail of a great garden at the foot of which appeared the glitter of a beautiful mansion struck by the sun, stood a pretty, fresh child, clad in those country garments' so full of affectation.

Luxury, freedom from care, and the habitual spectacle of wealth, make these children so pretty that one would think them formed of other paste than the sons of mediocrity or of poverty.

Beside him on the grass lay a splendid toy, fresh as its master, varnished, gilt, clad in a purple robe, covered with plumes and beads of glass. But the child was not occupied with his favored plaything, and this is what he was watching:

On the other side of the rail, on the road, among the thistles and the thorns, was another child, puny, dirty, fuliginous, one of those pariah-brats the beauty of which an impartial eye might discover if, as the eye of the connoisseur divines an ideal painting beneath the varnish of the coach-maker, it cleansed him of the repugnant patina of misery.

Across the symbolic bars which separate two worlds, the highway and the mansion, the poor child was showing the rich child his own toy, which the latter examined eagerly, as a rare and unknown object. Now, this toy, which the ragamuffin was provoking, tormenting, tossing in a grilled box, was a live rat! His parents, doubtless for economy, had taken the toy from life itself.

And the two children were laughing together fraternally, with teeth of equal *whiteness!*

THE GIFTS OF THE FAIRIES

It was that great assembly of the fairies, to proceed with the repartition of gifts among the new-born who had arrived at life within the last twenty-four hours.

All these antique and capricious sisters of destiny, all these bizarre mothers of sadness and of joy, were most diversified: some had a somber, crabbed air; others were wanton, mischievous; some, young, who had always been young; others old, who had always been old.

All the fathers who believed in fairies had come, each bearing his new-born in his arms.

Gifts, Faculties, Good Fortunes, Invincible Circumstances, were gathered at the side of the tribunal, as prizes on the platform for distribution. What was peculiar here was that the gifts were not the reward of an effort, but, quite the contrary, a grace accorded him who had not yet lived, a grace with power to determine his destiny and become as well the source of his misfortune as of his good.

The poor fairies were kept very busy; for the crowd of solicitors was great, and the intermediate world, placed between man and God, is subject, like man, to the terrible law of Time and his endless offspring, Days, Hours, Minutes, Seconds.

In truth, they were as bewildered as ministers on an audience day, or as guards at the Mont-de-Piété when a national holiday authorizes gratuitous liberations. I really think that from time to time they looked at the hands of the clock with as much impatience as human judges, who, sitting since morn, cannot help dreaming of dinner, of the family, and of their cherished slippers. If, in supernatural justice, there is a little of haste and of luck, we should not be surprised sometimes to find the same in human justice. We ourselves, in that case, would be unjust judges.

So some shams were enacted that day which might be thought bizarre, if prudence, rather than caprice, were the distinctive, eternal characteristic of the fairies.

For instance, the power of magnetically attracting fortune was awarded the sole heir of a very wealthy family, who, endowed with no feeling of charity, no more than with lust for the most visible goods of life, must later on find himself prodigiously embarrassed by his millions.

Thus, love of the beautiful and poetic power were given to the son of a gloomy knave, a quarry-man by trade, who could in no way develop the faculties or satisfy the needs of his deplorable offspring.

All the fairies rose, thinking their task was through; for there remained no gift, no bounty, to hurl at all that human fry, when one fine fellow, a poor little tradesman, I think, rose, and grasping by her robe of multicolored vapors the Fairy nearest at hand, cried:

"Oh, Madam! You are forgetting us! There is still my little one! I don't want to have come for nothing!"

The fairy could have been embarrassed, for there no longer was a thing. However, she recalled in time a law, well known, though rarely applied, in the supernatural world, inhabited by those impalpable deities, friends of man and often constrained to mold themselves to his passions, such as Fairies, Gnomes, Salamanders, Sylphides, Sylphs, Nixies, Watersprites and Undines —I mean the law which grants a Fairy, in a case similar to this, namely, in case of the exhausting of the prizes, power to give one more, supplementary and exceptional, provided always that she has sufficient imagination to create it at once.

Accordingly the good Fairy responded, with self-possession worthy of her rank: "I give to your son . . . I give him . . . *the gift of pleasing!*"

"Pleasing? How? Pleasing? Why?" obstinately asked the little shopkeeper, who was doubtless one of those logicians so commonly met, incapable of rising to the logic of the Absurd.

"Because! Because!" replied the incensed Fairy, turning her back on him; and, rejoining the train of her companions, she said to them: "What do you think of this little vainglorious Frenchman, who wants to know everything, and who, having secured for his son the best of gifts, dares still to question and to dispute the indisputable?"

SOLITUDE

A philanthropic journalist once said to me that solitude is harmful to man, and, to support his thesis, he cited—as do all unbelievers—words of the Christian Fathers.

I know that the Demon gladly frequents parched places, and that the spirit of murder and lechery is marvellously inflamed in solitude. But it is possible that solitude is dangerous only to the idle, rambling soul, who peoples it with his passions and his chimeras.

It is certain that a babbler, whose supreme pleasure consists in speaking from a pulpit or a rostrum, would be taking great chances of going stark mad on the island of Crusoe. I do not demand of my journalist the courageous virtues of Robinson, but I ask that he do not summon in accusation lovers of solitude and mystery.

There are in our chattering races individuals who would accept the supreme agony with less reluctance, if they were permitted to deliver a copious harangue front the height of the scaffold, without fear that the drums of Santerre[1] would unseasonably cut short their oration.

I do not pity them, for I guess that their oratorical effusions bring them delights equal to those which others draw from silence and seclusion; but I despise them.

I desire above all that my accursed journalist leave me to amuse myself as I will. "Then you never feel," he says in a very apostolic nasal tone, "the need of sharing your joys?" Do you see the subtle jealous one! He knows that I scorn his, and he comes to insinuate himself into mine, the horrible killjoy!

"The great misfortune of not being able to be alone," La Bruyère says somewhere, as though to shame those who rush to forget themselves in the crowd, fearing, doubtless, that they will be unable to endure themselves.

"Almost all our ills come to us from inability to remain in our room," said another sage, Pascal, I believe, recalling thus in the cell of meditation the frantic ones who seek happiness in animation, and in a prostitution which I could call fraternary, if I wished to use the fine language of my century.

PROJECTS

He said to himself, while strolling in the great lonely park: "How beautiful she would be in an intricate, gorgeous court costume, descending, through the air of a beauteous evening, the marble stairs of a palace, opposite shallow pools and great greenswards. For she has naturally the air of a princess."

Passing along a street somewhat later, he stopped before a print-shop, and finding in a portfolio an engraving of a tropical scene, he said: "No, it is not in a palace that I should like to be master of her beloved life. We would not feel at home. Besides, walls riddled with gold would afford no niche to hold her likeness; in those solemn galleries there is no intimate corner. Decidedly it is *there* I must live to develop the dream of my life."

And, analyzing the details of the engraving, he continued mentally: "At the edge of the sea, a little log cabin, surrounded by those shiny, bizarre trees, the names of which I have forgotten . . . in the air, an indefinable, intoxicating perfume . . . in the cabin, a potent fragrance of rose and of musk . . . farther off, behind our little domain, mast-tops swaying with the swell . . . around us, beyond the room lighted by a roseate glow sifted through the blinds, adorned with fresh matting and intoxicating flowers, with rare benches of Portuguese rococo, of a heavy and shadowy wood (where she will rest, so calm, so gently fanned, smoking tobacco tinged with opium), beyond the timbers of the ships, the racket of the birds drunk with the light, and the chattering of little negresses . . . and, at night, to serve as accompaniment to my musings, the plaintive song of musical trees, of melancholy beefwoods! Yes, in truth, there indeed is the setting that I seek. What have I to do with palaces?"

And still farther, as he followed a great avenue, he noticed a well-kept tavern, from a window of which, enlivened by curtains of checkered prints, two laughing heads leaned forth. And at once: "My fancy," he said, "must be a great vagabond to seek so far what is so near to me. Pleasure and good fortune are in the nearest tavern, in the chance tavern, so rich in happiness. A great fire, gaudy earthenware, a tolerable meal, rough wine, and an enormous bed with cloths somewhat coarse, but fresh; what more could be desired?"

And returning home, alone, at the hour when the counsels of Wisdom are not drowned by the hum of external life, he said: "I have had today, in my revery, three dwellings in which I have found equal pleasure. Why constrain my body to move about, when my soul voyages so freely? And to what end carry out projects, when the project itself is a sufficing joy?"

THE LOVELY DOROTHEA

The sun pours down upon the city with its direct and terrible light; the sand is dazzling, and the sea glistens. The stupefied world sinks cowardly down and holds siesta, a siesta which is a sort of delightful death, in which the sleeper, half-awake, enjoys the voluptuousness of his annihilation.

None the less, Dorothea, strong and proud as the sun, advances along the deserted street, alone animated at that hour, under the immense blue sky, forming a startling black spot against the light.

She advances, lightly, balancing her slender trunk upon her so large hips. Her close-fitting silk dress, of a clear, roseate fashion, stands out vividly against the darkness of her skin and is exactly molded to her long figure, her rounded back and her pointed throat.

Her red parasol, sifting the light, throws over her dark face the bloody disguise of its reflection.

The weight of her enormous, blue-black hair draws back her delicate head and gives her a triumphant, indolent bearing. Heavy pendants tinkle quietly at her delicate ears.

From time to time the sea-breeze lifts the hem of her flowing skirt and reveals her shining, superb limbs; and her foot, a match for the feet of the marble goddesses whom Europe locks in its museums, faithfully imprints its form in the fine sand. For Dorothea is such a wondrous coquette, that the pleasure of being admired overcomes the pride of the enfranchised, and, although she is free, she walks without shoes.

She advances thus, harmoniously, glad to be alive, smiling an open smile; as if she saw, far off in space, a mirrot reflecting her walk and her beauty.

At the hour when dogs moan with pain under the tormenting sun, what powerful motive can thus draw forth the indolent Dorothea, lovely, and cold as bronze?

Why had she left her little cabin, so coquettishly adorned, the flowers and mats of which make at so little cost a perfect boudoir; where she takes such delight in combing herself, in smoking, in being fanned, or in regarding herself in the mirror with its great fans of plumes; while the sea, which strikes the shore a hundred steps away, shapes to her formless reveries a mighty and monotonous accompaniment, and while the iron pot, in which a ragout of crabs with saffron and rice is cooking, sends after her, from the courtyard, its stimulating perfumes?

Perhaps she has a rendezvous with some young officer, who, on far distant shores, heard his comrades talk of the renowned Dorothea. Infallibly she will beg him, simple creature, to describe to her the Bal de l'Opera, and will ask him if one can go there barefoot, as to the Sunday dances, where the old Kaffir women themselves get drunk and mad with joy; and then, too, whether the lovely ladies of Paris are all lovelier than she.

Dorothea is admired and pampered by all, and she would be perfectly happy if she were not obliged to amass piastre on piastre to buy back her little sister, who is now fully eleven, and who is already mature, and so lovely! She will doubtless succeed, the good Dorothea; the child's master is so miserly, too miserly to understand another beauty than that of gold.

THE COUNTERFEIT MONEY

As we were moving away from the tobacconist's, my companion carefully sorted his money: in the left pocket of his waistcoat he slipped little gold pieces; in the right, little silver pieces; in the left pocket of his trousers, a mass of coppers, and finally, in the right, a silver two-franc pieces that he had particularly examined.

"Singular and minute distribution!" I said to myself.

We came across a pauper who, trembling, held forth his cap. I know nothing more disquieting than the dumb eloquence of those suppliant eyes which hold, for the sensitive man who can read within, both so great humility and so deep reproach. Something lies there which approaches that depth of complex feeling in the tearful eyes of dogs that are being flogged.

The offering of my friend was much more considerable than mine, and I said to him: "You are right; after the pleasure of being astonished, none is greater than that of creating a surprise." "It was the counterfeit," he answered tranquilly, as though to justify his prodigality.

But in my miserable brain, always busied seeking noon at two PM (of such a wearying faculty has nature made me a gift!), the idea suddenly came that such conduct, on the part of my friend, was excusable only by the desire to produce an occasion in the life of the poor devil, perhaps even to know the diverse consequences, disastrous or otherwise, that a counterfeit in the hands of a mendicant can engender. Could it not multiply itself in valid pieces? Could it not also lead him to jail? A tavern-keeper, a baker, for example, might perhaps have him arrested as a forger or a spreader of counterfeits. Quite as well the counterfeit coin might be, for a poor little speculator, the germ of a several days' wealth. And so my fancy ran its course, lending wings to the spirit of my friend and drawing all possible deductions from all imaginable hypotheses.

But he abruptly burst my revery asunder by taking up my own words: "Yes, you are right: there is no sweeter pleasure than to surprise a man by giving him more than he expected."

I looked into the whites of his eyes, and I was frightened to see that his eyes shone with an undeniable candor. I then saw clearly that he wished to combine charity and a good stroke of business; to gain forty sous and the heart of God; to sweep into Paradise economically; in short, to entrap gratis the brevet of charitable man.

I would almost have pardoned in him the desire of the criminal joy of which I had just now thought him capable! I would have thought it curious, singular, that he found it amusing to compromise the poor; but I shall never pardon the ineptitude of his calculation. One is never to be forgiven for being wicked, but there is some merit in being conscious that one is; the most irreparable of all evils is to do wrong through stupidity.

THE GENEROUS PLAYER

Yesterday, in the crowd of the boulevard, I felt myself grazed by a mysterious Being whom I have always wished to know, and whom I recognized at once, though I had never seen him. He doubtless had a similar wish to make my acquaintance, for he gave me a significant wink in passing which I hastened to obey. I followed him attentively, and soon I descended behind him into a resplendent subterranean abode, where sparkled a luxury that none of the better homes in Paris can nearly approach. It seemed odd to me that I could have passed by this enchanting den so often without divining the entrance. There reigned an exquisite, though heady atmosphere, which made one forget almost at once all the fastidious horrors of life; there one breathed a somber blessedness, similar to that which the lotus-eaters experienced when, disembarking on an enchanted isle, bright with the glimmerings of eternal afternoon, they felt growing within them, to the drowsy sound of melodious cascades, the desire never to see again their hearthstones, their wives, their children, and never to remount the high surges of the sea.

Strange visages of men and women were there, marked with a fatal beauty, which it seemed to me I had already seen in epochs and in lands I could not precisely recall, and which inspired me rather with a fraternal sympathy than with that fear which is usually born at sight of the unknown. If I wished to try to define in any way the singular expression of these visages, I should say that I had never seen eyes burning more feverishly with dread of ennui and with the immortal desire of feeling themselves alive.

My host and I were already, when we sat down, old and perfect friends. We ate, we drank beyond measure of all sorts of extraordinary wines, and—what was no less extraordinary—it seemed to me, after several hours, that I was no more drunken than he. Play, that superhuman pleasure, had meanwhile irregularly interrupted our frequent libations, and I must say that I staked and lost my soul, at the rubber, with heroic heedlessness and lightness. The soul is so impalpable a thing, so often useless and sometimes so annoying, that I experienced, at its loss, a little less emotion than if, on a walk, I had misplaced my visiting card. For a long time we smoked some cigars the incomparable savor and perfume of which gave the soul nostalgia for unknown lands and joys, and, intoxicated with all these delights, I dared, in an access of familiarity which seemed not to displease him, to cry, while mastering a cup full to the brim: "To your immortal health, old Buck!"

We talked, also, of the universe, of its creation and of its future destruction; of the great idea of the century, namely, progress and perfectibility; and, in general, of all forms of human infatuation. On this subject, His Highness never exhausted his fund of light and irrefutable pleasantries, and he expressed himself with an easy flow of speech and a quietness in his drollery that I have found in none of the most celebrated causeurs of humanity. He explained to me the absurdity of the different philosophies which have hitherto taken possession of the human brain, and deigned even to confide to me certain fundamental principles, the property and the benefits of which it does not suit me to share with the casual comer. He did not in any way bemoan the bad reputation which he enjoys in all parts of the world, assured me that he himself was the person most interested in the destruction of *superstition,* and confessed that he had never feared for his own power save once, on the day when he had heard a preacher, more subtle than his colleagues, cry from the pulpit: "My dear brethren, never forget, when you hear the progress of wisdom vaunted, that the cleverest ruse of the Devil is to persuade you he does not exist!"

The memory of this celebrated orator led us naturally to the subject of the academies, and my strange companion stated that he did not disdain, in many cases, to inspire the pen, the word, and the conscience of pedagogs, and that he was almost always present, though invisible, at the academic sessions.

Encouraged by so many kindnesses, I asked him for news of God, and whether he had recently seen Him. He answered, with a carelessness shaded with a certain sadness: "We greet one another when we meet, but as two old gentlemen, in whom an innate politeness cannot extinguish the memory of ancient bitterness."

It is doubtful that His Highness had ever granted so long an audience to a plain mortal, and I was afraid of abusing it. Finally, as the shivering dawn whitened the panes, this famous personage, sung by so many poets and served by so many philosophers who have worked unknowingly for his glory, said to me: "I want to leave you with a pleasant memory of me, and to prove that I, of whom so much ill is said, I can sometimes be a *good devil,* to make use of one of your common phrases. In order to compensate for the irremediable loss of your soul, I shall give you the stakes you would have won had fate been with you, namely, the possibility of reliev-ing and of conquering, all through your life, that odd affection of ennui which is the source of all your maladies and of all your wretched progress. Never shall a desire be framed by you which I will not aid you to realize; you shall reign over your vulgar fellow-men; you shall be stocked with flattery, even with adoration; silver, gold, diamonds, fairylike palaces, shall come seeking you and shall pray you to accept them, without your having made an effort to attain them; you shall change fatherland and country as often as your fancy may dictate; you shall riot in pleasures, unwearying, in charming countries where it is always warm and where the women are fragrant as the flowers—et cetera, et cetera . . ." he added, ris-ing and taking leave of me with a pleasant smile.

If I had not been afraid of humiliating myself before so vast an assemblage, I should gladly have fallen at the feet of this gen-erous player to thank him for his unheard of munificence. But little by little, after I had left him, incurable distrust reëntered my breast; I dared no longer believe in such prodigious good fortune, and, on going to bed, still saying my prayers through silly force of habit, I repeated in semi-slumber: "My God! Lord, my God! Let it be that the Devil keep his word!"

ENDNOTE

POEMS IN PROSE

SOLITUDE

[1] Santerre is the general of the French Revolution who ordered his drummers to play, drowning the words of Louis XVI from the scaffold.